Grand Diplôme Cooking Course

Volume 4

Grand Diplôme Cooking Course

A Danbury Press Book

The Danbury Press

a division of Grolier Enterprises, Inc.

Robert B. Clarke	Publisher
Robert G. Bartner	Marketing Director
Gilbert Evans	Creative Director
James W. Hinkley	Production Director

This book has been adapted from the Grand Diplôme Cooking Course, originally published by Purnell Cookery, U.S.A.

Purnell Grand Diplôme Editorial Board

Rosemary Hume and Muriel Downes
Principals:
London Cordon Bleu Cookery School

Anne Willan	Editor
Eleanor Noderer	Associate Editor
Sheryl Julian	Assistant Editor
John Paton	Managing Editor
José Northey	Co-ordinating Editor
Peter Leather	Art Editor
Charles F. Turgeon	Wine Consultant

Library of Congress Catalog Card Number: 72-13896
© B.P.C. Publishing, 1971, and
© Phoebus Publishing, 1972.
Filmsetting by Petty and Sons Ltd., Leeds, England.
Printed in the United States of America

234567899876543

All recipes have been tested either at the Cordon Bleu Cookery School in London or in our U.S. test kitchens.

Note: all recipe quantities in this book serve 4 people unless otherwise stated.

Contents

From the Editor

Classic French **Sautés** to suit sophisticates, ample **Main Course Salads** for weight-watchers, and melting **Meringues** that seduce the sweet tooth — there's something to please every taste in this fourth Volume of your Grand Diplôme Cooking Course, created by the London Cordon Bleu Cookery School.

Plan on **Poaching Fruits** when they are in season to drum up such delights as peach crêpes, apricot cheesecake, and rhubarb charlotte crowned with whipped cream. Master the old-fashioned skills of **Cooking with Milk**, and bake feather-light **Quick Breads, Muffins, Biscuits and Scones** that would make your grandmother proud.

For the housewife in a hurry there are **Casseroles** to tempt the epicure — halibut steaks baked with eggplant and tomatoes and spiked with capers; rock game hens cooked with red wine and gleaming with glazed onions; shellfish steamed together to make the famous San Franciscan cioppino. **Vegetables** take on new vitality in recipes like poor man's caviar — spiced eggplant purée from Turkey — and Provençal salad, a savory mixture of zucchini, tomatoes and bell peppers, seasoned with garlic.

Party entertaining is not forgotten and you have a choice of dinner **Menus** that feature loin of lamb portugaise stuffed with walnuts, roast duck Hymettus glazed with honey, and veal chops bonne femme baked with onions, mushrooms, potatoes and wine. Or, if you yearn for the outdoors, take a lavish picnic to please a crowd of hungry adults and children. You can cook it all before you go or add the finishing touches with an on-the-spot barbecue.

Have fun in and out of the kitchen. Bon Appétit!

Anne Willan

Savarin Chantilly, glistening with syrup, is ready to serve (recipe is on page 14)

SAVARIN SOAKED IN SYRUP

Melon salad is the simple start of a sumptuous menu of roast duck basted with honey, followed by savarin — a yeast cake soaked with liqueur and filled with whipped cream. An ideal companion for the roast duck is Châteauneuf-du-Pape, the most popular Rhône wine in America. Rather lighter than the other principal Rhône types, it has a generous bouquet and rich flavor. Petit Syrah is one of the grapes used in making Châteauneuf; when raised in California it produces a firm, full-bodied wine reminiscent of the Rhône.

Melon Salad
Hot Herb Loaf

Roast Duck Hymettus
Green Beans Béarnaise

Savarin Chantilly
or
Hot Chocolate

Soufflé Pudding

Red wine — Châteauneuf-du-Pape (Rhône)
or Petit Syrah (California)

TIMETABLE

Day before
Make stock from duck giblets and store in refrigerator. Make stuffing for duck and keep in a bowl in the refrigerator.
Make dressing for melon salad.

Morning
Stuff duck, truss and set in roasting pan ready for roasting.
Make and bake savarin. Soak with prepared syrup, cover and stand at room temperature.
Prepare melon salad and refrigerate.
Prepare herb loaf, wrap in foil and refrigerate.
Trim the beans, chop the onion, dice the bacon, and keep covered.

Assemble equipment for final cooking from 6:00 for dinner around 8 p.m.

Order of Work

6:00
Set oven at moderately hot (375°F).
Spread duck with honey and set in roasting pan.

6:15
Put duck in oven to roast.

6:45
Baste and turn duck.

7:15
Baste and turn duck again.
Make chocolate sauce; cover tightly to prevent a skin from forming.
Cook the green beans. Cook the onion for garnish, add bacon but do not heat.

Arrange the savarin on a platter and spoon over the liqueur. Whip the cream, sweeten to taste; add vanilla and pile in center of savarin. *Or make chocolate soufflé pudding.*

7:35
Drain the beans, refresh and leave in colander.

7:40
Start steaming pudding.
Stir chopped herbs into melon salad.

7:45
Remove duck from oven, transfer to a platter and keep hot; make gravy.

7:50
Put herb loaf in oven to heat.
Heat the onion and cook the bacon for the beans. Toss the beans with the onion and bacon until hot. Put in a serving dish.
Garnish duck with lemon slices, add watercress just before serving.

8:00
Take the loaf from the oven; serve with melon salad.
Draw steamer to side of stove and leave pudding to keep hot. Before serving dessert, reheat chocolate sauce and turn out pudding.

You will find that **cooking times** given in the individual recipes for these dishes have sometimes been adapted in timetable to help when cooking and serving this menu as a party meal.

Appetizer

Melon Salad

1 honeydew melon
3 medium tomatoes, peeled, seeded and cut in strips
2 cucumbers
salt
1 tablespoon chopped parsley
2 teaspoons chopped mint
2 teaspoons chopped chives

For vinaigrette dressing
2 tablespoons wine vinegar
salt and pepper
pinch of sugar
6 tablespoons oil

Method
Cut melon in half and remove seeds. Scoop out the fruit with a ball cutter or cut it into cubes, cut the melon shell in four and scrape clean; reserve.
Peel cucumbers and cut into cubes about the same size as the melon cubes, or smaller if you prefer. Sprinkle lightly with salt, cover with a plate and let stand for about 30 minutes. Then drain off all liquid, rinse the cubes under cold running water and dry on paper towels.
Make the vinaigrette dressing.
In a bowl combine fruit and vegetables, pour over dressing, cover and chill 2—3 hours.
Just before serving stir in the chopped herbs. Pile the salad into the reserved melon shells and eat it with a spoon because there is a lot of liquid. Serve it with hot herb loaf.

Cubes of melon, tomato and cucumber are combined with herbs and vinaigrette dressing for melon salad

Accompaniment to Appetizer

Hot Herb Loaf

1 loaf French bread
½ cup butter
1 tablespoon mixed herbs
   (basil, tarragon, oregano)
squeeze of lemon juice
black pepper
½ clove of garlic, crushed
   (optional)

Hot herb loaf is a delicious accompaniment to melon salad

Method
Cream the butter with the herbs, lemon juice, seasoning, and garlic if used.

Cut the bread into even, slanting slices about ½ inch thick almost but not quite through the base of the loaf. Spread each slice generously with butter mixture. Spread any remaining butter over top and sides of loaf and wrap in foil.

Bake in a hot oven (425°F) for 10 minutes. Reduce oven heat to 400°F, open foil and bake bread 5–8 minutes longer or until it is brown and crisp.

Succulent roast duck Hymettus is accompanied by green beans Béarnais and a rich gravy

Entrée

Roast Duck Hymettus

5 lb duck
1 teaspoon oil
2½ cups water
salt
1 onion, unpeeled
3 tablespoons honey
juice of ½ lemon
pepper
2 teaspoons arrowroot, mixed
    to a paste with 2 tablespoons
    water

For stuffing
2 tablespoons butter
1 medium onion, chopped
1 cup chopped walnuts or
    cashew nuts
1½ cups fresh white
    breadcrumbs
grated rind of 1 lemon
1 tablespoon chopped parsley
½ teaspoon sage
½ teaspoon thyme, or marjoram
½ teaspoon cinnamon
salt and pepper
1 egg, beaten to mix
juice of ½ lemon

For garnish
bunch of watercress
1 lemon, sliced

Trussing needle and string

Method
Set oven at moderately hot
(375°F).

To make the stock: in a
saucepan brown the duck
giblets, except the liver in 1
teaspoon oil. Add water, bring
to a boil and skim thoroughly.
Season mixture with salt and
add onion, washed and
trimmed but not peeled.
Simmer over low heat for
30—45 minutes. Strain.

To prepare the stuffing:
melt 1 tablespoon butter, add

chopped onion and cook
slowly until soft but not
browned. Add remaining
tablespoon butter to pan;
when melted, stir in the nuts
and fry until they are golden
brown. Transfer nuts and
onions to a bowl, add breadcrumbs, lemon rind and juice,
herbs and plenty of seasoning.
Add enough egg to bind the
mixture, put the stuffing into
cavity of duck and truss it
neatly.

Spread the duck with
honey, prick the skin and set
the bird on a rack in a roasting
pan. Roast in heated oven for
about 1½ hours. Baste and
turn from time to time, and
discard the excess fat from the
pan.

Lift duck from roasting pan,
remove trussing strings, trim
leg and wing bones and place
on a platter.

Discard the fat from pan,
but leave any brown solids or
sediment. Add strained lemon
juice and stock from the
giblets, with the chopped
duck liver, bring to a boil and
season to taste with salt and
pepper. Add arrowroot paste
and cook, stirring constantly,
until the gravy thickens. Strain,
reheat and taste for seasoning.

Garnish duck with water-
cress and lemon slices. Serve
gravy in a separate gravy boat.

The name **Hymettus** is
given to dishes that use
honey because Mount
Hymethus, near Athens,
Greece, is renowned for
its fine-tasting honey.

*Combine all ingredients for
the stuffing; add enough
beaten egg to bind mixture*

*Spread honey over the duck
after it has been stuffed and
trussed*

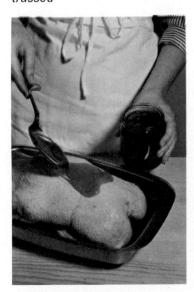

Accompaniment to Entrée

Green Beans Béarnaise

1 lb green beans, trimmed
4 slices of bacon
1 tablespoon butter
1 medium onion, finely
    chopped
black pepper, freshly ground

Method
Cook beans in plenty of boiling
salted water, without a lid, for
15—18 minutes or until barely
tender — there should be some
crispness left. Drain immediately and refresh under cold
running water; drain well.

Cut bacon into ½ inch strips
and set aside. Melt butter in a
skillet, add onion and cook
until tender but not brown.
Add bacon, increase heat and
fry until bacon is crisp and
onion brown. Discard the
excess fat, add the beans,
tossing frequently until hot.
Season with freshly ground
pepper.

*Mix the green beans, onion
and bacon just before serving*

Dessert

Savarin Chantilly

1½ cups flour
1 teaspoon salt
1 tablespoon sugar
3 tablespoons warm water
1 package dry yeast, or 1 cake
   compressed yeast
3 eggs
½ cup butter
syrup for basting

For Chantilly cream
1 cup heavy cream, stiffly
   whipped
½ teaspoon vanilla
3–4 teaspoons sugar (to taste)

*Ring, or savarin, mold
(3 cup capacity)*

Method

Sift flour into a bowl with the salt and sugar. Make a well in the center. In another bowl, sprinkle or crumble the yeast over warm water, stand 5 minutes, or until yeast is dissolved, and pour into the well. Add eggs and stir the mixture, gradually drawing in the flour until it is smooth. Beat with the hand for 5 minutes or until dough is very elastic, raising it up with the fingers and letting it fall back into the bowl. Cover bowl and stand in a warm place for 45–60 minutes, or until it has doubled in bulk. Set the oven at hot (400°F).

Cream the butter until soft and beat it into the dough until very smooth. Thoroughly butter the mold, spoon in the dough, cover and let stand again in a warm place until the dough rises to the top of the mold. Bake in heated oven for 25 minutes or until the savarin is brown and begins to shrink from the sides of the

mold.

Turn out onto a rack placed over a plate to catch excess syrup, and cool for a few minutes. While still warm, baste with the hot syrup. The savarin should be thoroughly soaked so it glistens and increases a good deal in size. Reheat the excess syrup and continue basting the savarin until all is absorbed.

To serve, transfer the savarin to a platter. Flavor the whipped cream with vanilla and sugar to taste, and pile it in the center of the savarin.

Syrup for Savarin

1½ cups sugar
2 cups water
2 strips lemon rind, thinly
   peeled, or ½ vanilla bean,
   split
2–3 tablespoons kirsch, or
   rum (optional)

Method

In a saucepan combine sugar and water and heat gently until sugar dissolves. Add lemon rind or vanilla bean; boil rapidly for 5 minutes, or until a drop of syrup tested between thumb and finger is sticky. Remove saucepan from heat and stir in the kirsch or rum, if you like. Remove lemon rind and vanilla bean and gradually spoon the hot syrup over the entire savarin. **Note:** if preparing the savarin ahead, do not add liqueur or rum to syrup; spoon it over the savarin just before serving.

1 For savarin, put sifted flour and sugar in a bowl, make a well in the center and add the yeast and water mixture

2 Stir the eggs into the yeast mixture; beat vigorously with the hand until the dough is elastic

3 Cover dough with a clean cloth and let stand in a warm place to rise

4 Add the creamed butter to the risen dough and beat until the mixture is very smooth

5 Pour the dough into a buttered savarin mold and let rise again to top of the mold

6 Place warm savarin on a wire rack over a plate and baste thoroughly with hot syrup until all is absorbed

Alternative Dessert

Hot Chocolate Soufflé Pudding

2 squares (2 oz) semisweet
  chocolate
1 tablespoon cocoa
1½ cups milk
3 tablespoons butter
3 tablespoons flour
3 tablespoons sugar
2 eggs
½ teaspoon vanilla

For chocolate sauce
2 squares (2 oz) semisweet
  chocolate, chopped
1 tablespoon cocoa
1½ cups water
2–3 tablespoons sugar
  (or to taste)
pinch of salt
½ teaspoon vanilla

*Charlotte mold or soufflé dish
(1 quart capacity)*

For a fluffier pudding, add 2 egg yolks to the mixture instead of 1 egg and 1 yolk and whip both egg whites.

Method
Grease the mold or soufflé dish and sprinkle it with sugar, discarding the excess.

Mix the cocoa with a little milk, then combine with the chocolate and the remaining milk in a saucepan. Heat gently, stirring, until the chocolate is melted, bring to a boil and cool slightly. Melt the butter in a pan, stir in the flour off the heat and add the chocolate milk. Bring to a boil, stirring, and simmer 1–2 minutes. Take from the heat and beat in the sugar with 1 egg and 1 egg yolk. Stir in the vanilla.

Beat the egg white until it holds a stiff peak and fold into the chocolate mixture. Pour the mixture into the prepared mold or dish, cover securely with buttered foil and place in a steamer or in a pan containing 1–2 inches of boiling water. Cover and steam 45–50 minutes or until the pudding is set, adding more boiling water to the pan as needed.

To make chocolate sauce: put the chopped chocolate in a pan and mix the cocoa with a little water. Add to the chocolate with the remaining water, sugar and salt. Heat gently, stirring, until the chocolate is melted and the sugar is dissolved, then simmer 10–12 minutes or until the sauce is the consistency of heavy cream. Add more sugar if necessary and stir in the vanilla.

Cool the pudding for 10 minutes, then turn out onto a warm platter and spoon over the sauce.

POACHING FRUIT

Peaches, apricots, plums and rhubarb are among the fruits that are delicious made into a compote — a term for fresh or dried fruit poached whole or in halves or quarters in a thick syrup to which flavorings may be added. Poaching must be done carefully so the syrup scarcely boils.

Too often, fruit is cooked haphazardly in a pan with water to cover, sugar is added at random, and then the fruit is boiled for an unmeasured length of time. The result is casually dismissed as 'only stewed fruit' — a justified criticism if it is overcooked and mushy with a watery syrup.

Preparation of Fruit

Pick over the fruit and cut out any bruised flesh, then wash in a colander under cold running water.

Peaches, apricots and large plums. Split them by running a stainless steel knife around the fruit from the stalk end, following the slight indentation, and cutting through to the pit. Give the fruit a slight twist and separate the halves so the pit can be removed.

If the pits do not come out easily, cook the fruit whole and detach them after cooking.

Place the fruit, rounded side down, in a pan with syrup and bring very slowly to a boil. Let syrup boil up and over the fruit and then reduce the heat, cover the pan and leave to simmer very gently until tender. Cool the fruit slightly, then peel the skin from peaches or apricots – this should be easy to do after the fruit is cooked.

Even fruit that is fully ripe must be cooked thoroughly to allow syrup to penetrate and sweeten it and to prevent discoloration.

Rhubarb. Wash and dry the rhubarb and cut into even lengths. For every $1-1\frac{1}{2}$ lb rhubarb, spread 2 tablespoons of red currant jelly or strained rapsberry jam over the bottom and sides of a small casserole, add the rhubarb and put 1 more tablespoon of jelly or jam on top. Cover the pan and poach in a moderate oven (350°F) for 30 minutes or until tender. Or cut in even lengths and cook like apricots and plums.

Cranberries. Add the fruit to the sugar syrup and bring to a boil over medium heat. Simmer 2–3 minutes or until the cranberries are just tender. When serving cranberries as a compote, overcook them so they burst. Add extra sugar to taste and let cool.

Syrup. When cooking fruit, it is important that the water and sugar are made into a syrup before the fruit is added. The usual proportion for this syrup is $1\frac{1}{2}$ cups of water to 6 tablespoons of sugar for each lb of fruit. Heat the syrup gently in a pan to dissolve the sugar and boil rapidly for 2 minutes before the fruit is added. The syrup may be flavored with lemon rind or a vanilla bean.

Watchpoint: do not add any extra sugar to the fruit even if it is very sour, since too thick a syrup tends to toughen the skins of some fruit while cooking. If the fruit is excessively sour, add extra sugar after fruit is cooked but still hot.

Langues de chats or **cats' tongues cookies** take their name from their shape — thin, flat and narrow like a cat's tongue. They are served with sparkling wines and iced desserts and are also used as an ingredient for various desserts. If they are not available, use ladyfingers or Champagne cookies.

Peach Charlotte

1 lb fresh peaches, halved and pitted
sugar syrup (made with 1 cup water and $\frac{1}{4}$ cup sugar)
3 tablespoons sugar
1 envelope gelatin
6 tablespoons water
1 cup heavy cream, whipped until it holds a soft shape

To serve
$\frac{1}{2}$ cup heavy cream, stiffly whipped
1 package cats' tongues cookies, or ladyfingers

Charlotte mold, or soufflé dish (5 cup capacity); pastry bag and a medium star tube

Method
Lightly oil the mold or dish. Make sugar syrup and poach the peaches in it until tender. Strain and reserve the syrup.

Keep 1 peach half for decoration and rub remainder through a sieve, or peel them and purée in a blender. Measure this purée and add enough syrup to make 2 cups. Stir in the sugar. Sprinkle gelatin over the water and leave 5 minutes until spongy; dissolve over a pan of hot water and stir into the peach purée.

Pour peach mixture into a saucepan, stand this in a bowl of cold water with a few ice cubes added and stir until the mixture begins to thicken. Fold the stiffly whipped cream into the mixture and pour into the prepared mold or dish. Cover and chill about 2 hours or until set.

To serve, turn out the charlotte, spread the stiffly whipped cream over the cats' tongues or ladyfingers, and overlap them around the sides of the charlotte. This makes the cookies fit better and stops the cream from

oozing out between them.

Fill the remaining cream into the pastry bag fitted with the star tube and decorate the top with rosettes of cream and the reserved peach half, cut into slices.

Peach Crêpes

1 lb small fresh peaches, halved and pitted
sugar syrup (made with $1\frac{1}{2}$ cups water, 6 tablespoons sugar and peeled rind of $\frac{1}{2}$ lemon)
2 tablespoons apricot jam, sieved
juice of $\frac{1}{2}$ lemon
2 tablespoons slivered almonds, toasted (optional)

For crêpe batter
1 cup flour
pinch of salt
1 egg
1 egg yolk
$1\frac{1}{2}$ cups milk
2 tablespoons oil, or melted butter
oil (for frying)

6 inch crêpe pan, or skillet

Method
Make the sugar syrup and poach the peaches in it.

To prepare crêpe batter: sift flour with salt into a bowl, add egg and egg yolk and gradually stir in half the milk. Beat well, add oil or melted butter and whisk in remaining milk. Let stand 30 minutes before frying small, paper-thin crêpes.

To fry crêpes: heat pan and add 2–3 drops of oil. Pour about 2–3 tablespoons batter into the pan, immediately tilting it in a circle to coat the bottom evenly. Cook the crêpe $\frac{1}{2}$ minute or until the underneath is golden brown, then toss or flip over and cook 3–5 seconds longer or until brown. Cook remaining batter

in same way.

Stack crêpes on top of each other on a rack until needed. If they are to be kept for a few hours or overnight, wrap them in foil or a plastic bag.

Lift peaches from the pan with a slotted spoon, peel and cut into slices. Add jam and lemon juice to the syrup and stir over gentle heat until jam is melted. Boil 5 minutes, or until the sauce is thick and syrupy. Strain.

Layer crêpes with the peaches in a buttered oven-proof dish, starting and finishing with a crêpe. Cut into wedges like a cake; spoon over the jam sauce.

Bake the dish in a hot oven (400°F) for 10 minutes or until brown and crisp. Scatter almonds on top and serve.

Peaches Alsacienne

4 large fresh peaches, halved and pitted
sugar syrup, made with 1 cup water and $\frac{1}{4}$ cup sugar
$\frac{1}{4}$ cup slivered almonds, browned (see box, page 106)

For custard
$1\frac{1}{4}$ cups heavy cream
3 egg yolks
$\frac{1}{4}$ cup sugar
1 tablespoon cornstarch
2 tablespoons kirsch

Method
In a small deep pan, make the sugar syrup. Poach the peaches in it, one by one, for 2–3 minutes or until tender. Lift out the peaches, let cool slightly and remove the skins. Boil the syrup until it is reduced to $\frac{1}{2}$ cup.

To make the custard: scald $\frac{3}{4}$ cup of the cream. In a bowl beat the egg yolks with the sugar until thick and light.

Stir in the cornstarch, then add the scalded cream and the peach syrup and stir until mixed. Return the mixture to the pan and bring to a boil, stirring. Simmer 2 minutes and let cool; tightly cover to prevent a skin from forming.

Whip the remaining cream until it holds a stiff peak and fold it into the custard with the kirsch. Set the peaches in individual serving bowls and spoon the custard over them. Sprinkle with browned almonds.

Peaches Flambé

1½ lb fresh peaches, halved
    and pitted
sugar syrup, made with 1½ cups
    water and ¼ cup sugar
3 tablespoons butter
¼ cup brown sugar
3 tablespoons brandy or rum
3 tablespoons orange liqueur
    such as Grand Marnier,
    Curaçao or Triple Sec

Traditionally this dish is flamed in a chafing dish at the table.

Method
Make the sugar syrup and poach the peaches in it, one by one, for about 2 minutes or until barely tender. Lift out the peaches, let cool slightly and remove the skins. Boil the syrup until it is reduced to ¾ cup.

In a chafing dish melt the butter, add the peach halves and pour over the peach syrup. Sprinkle with the brown sugar and cook, basting constantly, until the peaches are lightly browned with caramelized sugar.

Add the brandy or rum and orange liqueur and flame, basting constantly with the flaming syrup. Serve at once.

Rhubarb fool — whipped cream stirred into the rhubarb mixture gives a marbled effect

Rhubarb Fool

1 lb fresh rhubarb
sugar syrup (made with ½ cup
 water and 2 tablespoons
 sugar)
1 tablespoon sugar (or to taste)
¾ cup thick custard (made with
 3 egg yolks and ¾ cup milk)
¾ cup heavy cream, whipped
 until it holds a soft shape

To serve
ladyfingers, or crisp cookies

Method
Make sugar syrup. Prepare
rhubarb and cook in the syrup;
drain and work through a
nylon strainer into a bowl.
Sweeten to taste with sugar
and chill.

To prepare the custard:
beat egg yolks in a bowl and
gently heat the milk in a
saucepan (do not boil).
Gradually pour the milk onto
the egg yolks, stirring constantly, and strain back into
the rinsed pan. Stir gently
over low heat until the mixture thickens and just coats
the back of a wooden spoon.
Do not boil as it will curdle.
Chill.

When cold, combine with
the rhubarb purée. Fold the
lightly whipped cream into
the rhubarb mixture, then stir
lightly to give a marbled
effect.

Serve in sherbet glasses or
in a glass bowl, with either
ladyfingers or crisp cookies.

Rhubarb Charlotte

1 lb rhubarb
¼ cup red currant jelly, or
 strained raspberry jam
1 envelope gelatin
¼ cup water
1 egg white
¼ cup sugar
1 cup heavy cream, whipped
 until it holds a soft shape

To serve
½ cup heavy cream, stiffly
 whipped
1 package cats' tongues, or
 ladyfingers

*Charlotte mold, or soufflé dish
(1 quart capacity); pastry bag
and a medium star tube*

Method
Set oven at moderate (350°F).
Wet the mold or dish.

Wash and dry rhubarb; cut
into even lengths. Spread 2
tablespoons jelly or jam over
bottom and sides of a casserole, add rhubarb; cover
with remaining jelly or jam.
Cover; poach in heated oven
for 30 minutes or until tender.
Work through a nylon sieve
or purée in a blender and cool.

In a small pan sprinkle
gelatin over water and leave
5 minutes until spongy, then
dissolve over a pan of hot
water; stir into rhubarb purée.
Place egg white in a small
bowl and beat until stiff; beat
in sugar gradually until mixture holds a soft shape. Fold
in the lightly whipped cream.
When the purée is cold and
beginning to thicken, fold in
cream mixture. Pour at once
into the mold or dish, cover
with foil and chill 2 hours or
until set.

To serve, turn charlotte out
onto a flat platter. Spread the
stiffly whipped cream over
the cats' tongues, or ladyfingers, and overlap them
around the sides of the charlotte. Fill the remaining cream
into the pastry bag fitted with
the star tube and decorate
the top with rosettes of cream.

Plum Suédoise

1½ lb fresh prune plums, halved
 and pitted
sugar syrup (made with 1½ cups
 water and ½ cup sugar)
1 envelope gelatin
few blanched almonds

*Deep 6 inch soufflé dish, or
 charlotte mold (1 quart
 capacity)*

Method
Make sugar syrup and poach
the plums in it; cook for at
least 15 minutes to develop
their flavor. Drain the fruit,
reserving the syrup and a
few of the best halves. Work
the remaining plum halves
through a nylon sieve or purée
them in a blender.

Measure 2 cups of syrup
and add 1½ cups to the fruit
purée. Sprinkle gelatin over
the remaining ½ cup syrup and
stand 5 minutes until spongy;
dissolve over a pan of hot
water, then add to the purée.
Chill over a pan of ice water,
stirring occasionally.
Watchpoint: if using plums
that are very acid, more
gelatin may be needed.

Put half a blanched almond
in each reserved plum half
and arrange at the bottom
of the wet mold, cut sides
down.

When purée is at the point
of setting, carefully pour into
the mold. Chill 2 hours or
until set.

Turn out mold and serve
with whipped cream or crème
à la vanille (vanilla custard
sauce).

Crème à la Vanille (Vanilla Custard Sauce)

1 cup milk, or half and half
1½ tablespoons sugar
½ teaspoon vanilla extract,
 or ½ vanilla bean, split
2 egg yolks

Method
Put milk in a pan with sugar
and heat until dissolved; if
using vanilla bean, infuse it
in the milk for 10 minutes,
keeping pan covered. Take
out bean, then add the sugar.

Beat egg yolks in a bowl
until lightly colored, scald
the vanilla-flavored milk and
gradually stir into yolks.
Return to pan and stir with a
wooden spoon over gentle
heat. When custard coats
back of spoon and looks
creamy, strain back into bowl.
Add the vanilla if using.
Sprinkle with a little sugar
and cool. This coating of
sugar melts and helps to
prevent a skin from forming.
Watchpoint: if the custard
gets too hot and starts to
curdle, pour it at once into
the bowl without straining
and whisk briskly for 10
seconds. Remember that
cooking over a gentle heat
helps to prevent a custard
from curdling and makes it
creamier.

Plum Condé

1 lb fresh prune plums, pitted
sugar syrup (made with
   $1\frac{1}{2}$ cups water and
   6 tablespoons sugar)
6 tablespoons round grain rice
$2\frac{1}{2}$ cups milk
1 tablespoon sugar
$\frac{1}{2}$ teaspoon vanilla
1 envelope gelatin
1 tablespoon cold water
5 tablespoons plum syrup
   (reserved from poaching
   plums)
$\frac{1}{2}$ cup heavy cream, whipped
   until it holds a soft shape
1 egg white

*Bundt pan, or ring mold (4–5
cup capacity)*

Method
Wet the pan or mold. Make the sugar syrup and poach the plums in the syrup until tender. Chill.

Meanwhile wash rice in a strainer under cold running water and drain well.

Bring milk to a boil, add rice and cook gently, stirring occasionally to prevent it from sticking.

Sprinkle gelatin over the cold water, add the 5 tablespoons of plum syrup and stand 5 minutes or until spongy.

Test the rice after 25–30 minutes and, when very soft and nearly all the milk has been absorbed, remove from the heat. Add sugar and vanilla, stir in the gelatin until it is dissolved, and put into a bowl to cool.

Whisk the egg white until it holds a stiff peak. When the rice mixture is cool, fold in the lightly whipped cream and egg white and pour the mixture into the pan or mold. Cover and chill 2 hours or until set.

Turn the mold out onto a platter. Drain the plums and arrange in the center. Any remaining plums may be pushed through a nylon sieve, or puréed in a blender and thinned with a little plum syrup to make a sauce. Spoon this carefully over the plums or serve separately in a sauce boat.

Cranberry Orange Relish

4 cups (1 lb) cranberries
grated rind and juice of
   1 orange
sugar syrup, made with 1 cup
   water and 6 tablespoons
   sugar
$1\frac{1}{2}$ cups sugar
$\frac{1}{2}$ cup slivered almonds
   (optional)

Serve with turkey and cold meats.

Method
Make the sugar syrup, add the cranberries and bring to a boil. Cook, without stirring, for 8–10 minutes or until the cranberries burst.

Take from the heat, stir in the remaining sugar, orange rind and juice and skim any scum from the top of the mixture. Let cool and stir in the almonds, if using.

Cranberry Sherbet

4 cups (1 lb) cranberries
sugar syrup, made with
   $1\frac{1}{2}$ cups water and
   6 tablespoons sugar
1 cup sugar
2 tablespoons sherry
1 envelope gelatin
$\frac{1}{4}$ cup water
1 egg white

Method
Make the sugar syrup, add the cranberries and bring to a boil. Simmer 2–3 minutes or until the cranberries are just tender. Stir in the remaining sugar and sherry.

Sprinkle the gelatin over the water and let stand 5 minutes until spongy. Stir into the hot cranberry mixture until dissolved. Let cool, then pour the mixture into ice trays and freeze, with the freezer turned to maximum coldness, until the mixture is slushy. Stiffly whip the egg white.

Turn the cranberry mixture into a chilled bowl, beat with a chilled beater until smooth, then beat in the egg white. Cover tightly with foil or wax paper; chill again, beating once or twice more to break up the ice crystals as the sherbet freezes.

When very firm, pack into chilled molds or glasses, or leave in the ice trays, tightly covered, until ready to serve. Turn the freezer back to normal setting.

Apricot Cheesecake

$\frac{1}{2}$ lb fresh apricots, halved and
   pitted
sugar syrup (made with $\frac{3}{4}$ cup
   water and 3 tablespoons
   sugar)
2 tablespoons melted butter
1 cup zwieback crumbs
1 lb cottage cheese
$\frac{1}{4}$ cup butter
$\frac{1}{2}$ cup sugar
1 large or 2 small eggs,
   well beaten
$\frac{1}{2}$ teaspoon vanilla

7 inch springform pan

If fresh apricots are not available, use canned ones.

Method
Set oven at moderate (350°F).

Make sugar syrup and poach apricots in it. Mix 2 tablespoons melted butter with most of zwieback crumbs and press over bottom and sides of pan.

Work the cottage cheese through a sieve, cream the $\frac{1}{4}$ cup butter and gradually beat in sugar until the mixture is soft and light. Add the cheese with the egg. Beat until light and fluffy; flavor with vanilla. Carefully spoon mixture into prepared pan, smooth the top with a palette knife and scatter with remaining crumbs. Bake in heated oven for 45–55 minutes or until firm.

Leave overnight or at least 4 hours before removing from pan. Drain apricots and arrange on top of the cake. Boil the syrup until thick and spoon over the apricots.

Apricot flan — one of many ways of using poached fruit

Apricot Flan

1 lb fresh apricots, halved and
    pitted
sugar syrup (made with 1 cup
    water and 6 tablespoons
    sugar)
$\frac{3}{4}$ cup apricot jam glaze
    (see Volume 1)

For rich pie pastry
$1\frac{1}{2}$ cups flour
pinch of salt
9 tablespoons butter
1 tablespoon sugar
1 egg yolk
2 tablespoons cold water

7—8 inch flan ring

Method
Make the pastry dough and
chill.

Make the sugar syrup, and
poach the apricots in it until
they are tender. Cool them in
the syrup slightly, then peel.

Roll out the pastry dough,
line the flan ring and bake
blind. Cool on a wire rack.

Brush a light coating of
apricot jam glaze over the
bottom and sides of the pastry
shell. Lift the apricots from
the syrup and arrange them
in the shell. Brush well with
hot apricot jam glaze. Let cool
before serving.
Note: the apricot syrup can

be thickened and used in
place of a jam glaze, but jam
is better if the flan has to be
kept for a while before serving.

If you like, decorate the
flan with whipped cream.

23

Deviled tuna salad is garnished with sieved egg yolk, cucumber slices and chopped egg white (recipe is on page 26)

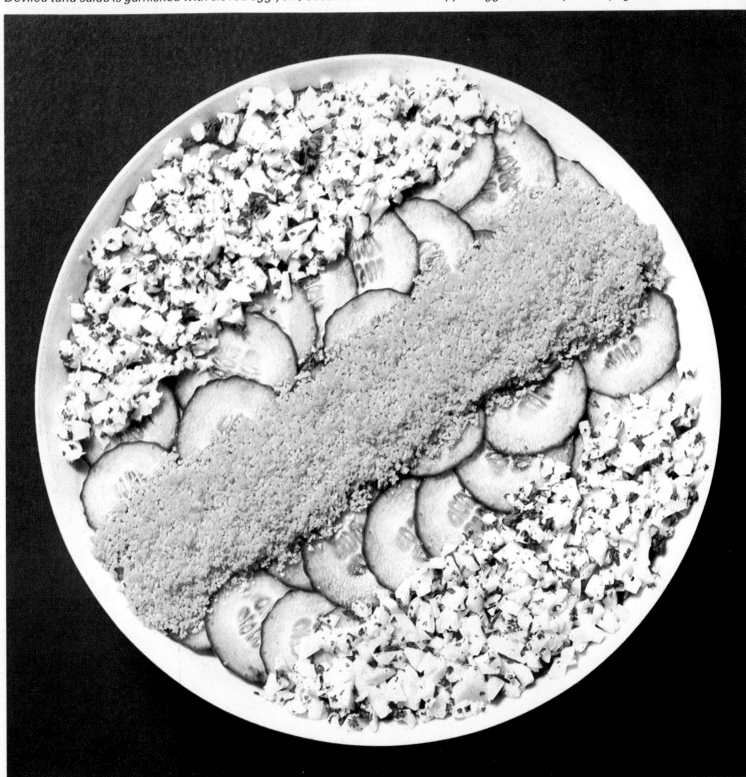

MAIN COURSE SALADS

Salads are an effortless entrée, and can be a good way of using up leftovers or improvising with cans from the cupboard.

If using leftover meat, slice or dice it neatly and marinate it in a little vinaigrette dressing, even if the salad is to be coated with mayonnaise. This gives moistness and flavor to the meat. As a general rule, salads of cooked meat or vegetables can be made in advance and left to marinate in the dressing for several hours — the flavors will mellow and improve. However, a delicate fresh vegetable like lettuce must be dressed at the last minute because it becomes limp quickly.

Be careful when adding mayonnaise — it will hold up for a few hours in a mixed salad that is stored, covered, in the refrigerator, but mayonnaise that is used for coating eggs, for example, quickly acquires a yellow skin as it stands. Such salads should be served within an hour.

Deviled Tuna Salad

1 can (9¼ oz) tuna
2 cups (1 lb) green beans
1 cucumber
1 teaspoon sugar

For dressing
2 tablespoons red wine
   vinegar
2 teaspoons Dijon-style
   mustard
¼ cup tomato ketchup
6 tablespoons olive oil
salt and pepper

For garnish
2 hard-cooked eggs and
   2 teaspoons chopped parsley,
   or 8 anchovy fillets and
   8 ripe olives, pitted

Method

Drain tuna and flake carefully with two forks. Mix vinegar, mustard and ketchup and whisk in the oil. Season to taste and spoon this sauce over the tuna. Leave to marinate while preparing the vegetables and garnish.

Trim beans and cut into thick diagonal slices. Cook in boiling salted water until just tender, drain, refresh under cold running water and drain again. Peel the cucumber and slice it; sprinkle lightly with salt and leave pressed between two plates for 30 minutes. Rinse cucumber under cold water; drain. Sprinkle slices with sugar and pepper to taste.

Put a layer of beans at the bottom of a shallow serving dish. Cover with a layer of the deviled tuna and repeat the layers until the dish is full, ending with the tuna. Cover with sliced cucumber.

To garnish: either decorate the top with bands of egg white, chopped and mixed with parsley, and egg yolk worked through a wire sieve, or make a lattice of anchovies and ripe olives on top of the cucumber.

Shrimp Salad

¾ lb peeled, cooked shrimps
1 cantaloupe, Persian or
   honeydew melon
4 large tomatoes, peeled and
   sliced
1 teaspoon sugar
½ cup vinaigrette dressing
1 head of Boston, or romaine,
   lettuce
1½ tablespoons mixed chopped
   herbs (parsley, thyme, chives
   and mint)

For dressing
1 teaspoon dry mustard
1 cup mayonnaise

Method

Cut the melon in half and discard the seeds. Scoop out the flesh with a ball cutter or cut into cubes. Mix with the shrimps and reserve. Arrange tomatoes, overlapping, around a serving dish or salad bowl. Sprinkle with sugar and spoon over a little of the vinaigrette dressing. Shred the lettuce very finely and place in the middle of the dish.

Add mixed herbs to remaining vinaigrette dressing and pour it over shrimps and melon: pile mixture on top of lettuce.

Mix the mustard to a paste with a little water and stir into the mayonnaise with enough boiling water to make a pourable dressing. Serve separately.

Salmon Salad en Gelée

1½ lb fresh salmon
4 cups water
juice of 1 lemon
1 teaspoon salt
6 white peppercorns
bouquet garni

For wine aspic
5 cups jellied chicken stock
   (the cooking broth from a
   boiled chicken, flavored
   with onion, carrot, and
   celery)
salt and pepper
1 envelope gelatin
1 cup dry white wine
2 teaspoons tarragon vinegar
2 egg whites
3 tablespoons chopped parsley

To serve
¼ cup heavy cream, whipped
   until it holds a soft shape
1 cup mayonnaise

*Glass serving bowl, or mold
(2 quart capacity)*

Method

Wash fish and dry well. Bring water and flavorings to a boil, draw aside and stand 5 minutes. Put salmon into the hot liquid, cover and bring slowly to a boil again. Poach for 10 minutes or until fish flakes easily when tested with a fork.

Watchpoint: the water must just tremble, not boil, during cooking, or the salmon will become tough.

Cool fish slightly, drain and remove skin and bones.

To make the wine aspic: be sure chicken stock is free of fat and seasoned very well. If it is not jellied, add another envelope of gelatin. Sprinkle gelatin over the wine and stand 5 minutes until spongy.

To clarify aspic: pour cold stock into a large saucepan and add vinegar. Whisk egg whites to a froth and add to chicken stock. Bring mixture slowly to a boil, whisking fast at first, then more slowly as the whites cook and look milky. When the stock is hot add the gelatin and continue whisking steadily until the mixture boils. Stop whisking and let mixture rise to the top of the pan. Take from the heat and leave to settle for 5 minutes, then bring to a boil again and let settle. Cool 10 minutes.

Have a dish towel or cloth soaked in boiling water ready. Spread it over a bowl and gently ladle the aspic and egg mixture into it. The liquid that drains through should be clear and sparkling. Lift the cloth without squeezing it and leave ½–1 hour so all the liquid drains. Cool it. More detailed instructions for making aspic will be given in a future Volume.

Flake salmon carefully and place it in a glass serving bowl or mold. Add enough cold but still liquid aspic to cover, and chill until set. Add parsley to remaining aspic and, when cool and on the point of setting, pour carefully into the bowl. Chill until set. Serve in the glass bowl or turn out of the mold and garnish with lettuce leaves. If aspic is to be unmolded, add another envelope of gelatin to the mixture so that it sets firmly.

Mix the lightly whipped cream with the mayonnaise and serve separately.

Sardine Salad

2 cans sardines, in oil
1 medium onion, grated
4 medium tomatoes, peeled
  and sliced
3 tablespoons capers
6 tablespoons vinaigrette
  dressing
1½ tablespoons chopped
  parsley

Method

Drain sardines, split them and remove the backbones.

Put a layer of sliced tomatoes in a shallow serving dish, sprinkle with half the grated onion and half the capers and cover with a layer of sardines. Arrange remaining tomatoes in a layer on top, cover with remaining onion, capers and sardines.

Spoon over the vinaigrette dressing and sprinkle the top with chopped parsley.

Stuffed Eggs Aurore

8 hard-cooked eggs
½ cup butter, softened
3 slices of canned pimiento
salt and pepper
1 cup mayonnaise
3 tomatoes
1½ teaspoons tomato paste
dash of Tabasco
bunch of watercress
  (to garnish)
buttered wholewheat bread
  (to serve)

Method

Halve eggs lengthwise, remove yolks and beat them with the butter; cover whites with cold water and reserve. Chop the pimiento and work through a fine sieve or purée in a blender. Beat into the yolks and butter mixture. Season well and soften, if necessary, with about 1 teaspoon mayonnaise.

Scald and peel tomatoes and slice two of them. Quarter the other, scoop out the seeds, reserve, and cut the flesh in fine strips.

Season the mayonnaise with the tomato paste and Tabasco, and thin to a coating consistency with a little juice strained from the tomato seeds. Drain egg whites and dry on paper towels. Cut a thin slice from the base of each egg so it sits firmly, fill the egg halves with the yolk and pimiento mixture and press the halves together.

Arrange the eggs on a platter and coat each with a spoonful of mayonnaise. Arrange the tomato slices, overlapping, around the eggs and put a spoonful of tomato strips on top of each egg.

Garnish the dish with watercress and serve with buttered wholewheat bread.

Egg and Beet Salad

6 hard-cooked eggs
4 large cooked beets, or
  1 can (1 lb) sliced beets
10–12 small new potatoes
6 scallions, chopped
½ cup boiled dressing or
  mayonnaise

For horseradish cream
1 tablespoon grated fresh
  horseradish, or 2 tablespoons
  prepared horseradish
1 tablespoon sugar
1½ teaspoons dry mustard
½ teaspoon salt
black pepper, freshly ground
2 tablespoons wine vinegar
¼ cup heavy cream

Method

Skin and slice cooked beets, or drain canned beets. Scrub or peel potatoes and cook in boiling salted water for 15–20 minutes or until just tender. Drain.

To make the horseradish cream: mix sugar and mustard with vinegar; stir in horseradish and cream, and season to taste.

If potatoes are very small, leave them whole; otherwise quarter or slice them, and mix while still warm with the horseradish cream and the chopped scallions. Mix in the sliced beets and pile in the center of a serving dish. Halve the eggs, arrange around the edge and coat each egg with a spoonful of boiled dressing or mayonnaise.

Cervelat Salad

1 lb cervelat or summer
  sausage, thinly sliced
1 Bermuda or other mild
  onion, thinly sliced
2 hard-cooked eggs, cut in
  wedges
2 tomatoes, peeled and cut
  in 8 wedges
3 dill pickles, cut in quarters
  lengthwise
1 tablespoon chopped parsley
  (for garnish)

For dressing
2 teaspoons prepared mustard
2 cloves of garlic, crushed
2 tablespoons mayonnaise
salt and pepper
½ cup cider vinegar
½ cup oil

Method

To make the dressing: stir the mustard and garlic into the mayonnaise with the seasoning. Stir in the vinegar, then gradually whisk in the oil so the dressing emulsifies and thickens slightly. Taste for seasoning.

Arrange the sausage and onion slices overlapping in a dish, spoon over the dressing, cover and let marinate for 2–8 hours.

A short time before serving, arrange the eggs, tomatoes and dill pickles around the dish. Sprinkle with chopped parsley.

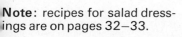

Note: recipes for salad dressings are on pages 32–33.

Egg and beet, and corned beef salads are substantial enough for a main dish

Corned Beef Salad

1 lb corned beef
4 large potatoes
¾ cup mayonnaise
1 large dill pickle, chopped
2 Bibb or 1 firm Boston lettuce
2 hard-cooked eggs, quartered

For mustard dressing
1 tablespoon dry mustard
1½ tablespoons dark brown
  sugar
3 tablespoons cider vinegar

Method
Cut beef in julienne strips.
Boil potatoes in their skins.

To make the mustard dressing: mix mustard and sugar
with the vinegar and stir until
dissolved.

Peel potatoes while still
hot; slice a layer into a serving
dish. Spread with a thin coating of mayonnaise and
sprinkle with a little chopped
pickle. Cover with a layer of
beef and moisten with some
of the mustard dressing.

Continue in this way until all
the ingredients are used,
ending with beef.

Wash the lettuce, remove
outer leaves and halve the
Bibb, or quarter the Boston
lettuce. Garnish the salad with
the lettuce heart and quarters
of hard-cooked eggs.

*Chop the dill pickle before
adding to corned beef salad*

Beef Salad

1 lb cold cooked roast beef,
  preferably rare
1 large dill pickle, sliced
9–12 ripe olives, halved and
  pitted
3 tomatoes, peeled, seeded
  and cut in strips
8 slices of French bread

For dressing
2 teaspoons paprika
1 teaspoon dry mustard
1 clove of garlic, crushed
2 tablespoons red wine vinegar
salt
black pepper, freshly ground
6 tablespoons olive oil

Method
Cut beef in ¼ inch slices and
then into julienne strips.

To make dressing: mix
paprika, mustard, garlic, and
vinegar with salt and pepper
to taste, then whisk in the oil.
When the dressing is emulsified, pour it over the beef and
leave to marinate.

Place the French bread on

a platter and pile a spoonful
of the beef and dressing on
each slice. Top with the tomatoes and decorate with the
sliced pickle and olives.

Pork Salad

1 lb cold roast pork, or cold
  cooked smoked pork
1½ cups finely shredded
  cabbage
3 tablespoons olive oil
3 dessert apples, pared and
  thinly sliced
1½ tablespoons chopped
  chives, or parsley

For cider cream dressing
3 tablespoons cider
1 teaspoon Dijon-style mustard
salt
black pepper, freshly ground
¾ cup heavy cream

Method
Dice the pork. Put cabbage in
a large bowl, sprinkle with
olive oil and toss with 2
wooden spoons until every

shred is coated with oil. Add the sliced apple.

Mix mustard and salt and pepper to taste with the cider and whisk in the cream. Add pork to the cabbage, spoon over the cider cream dressing and pile in a serving dish. Sprinkle with chives or parsley.

Louis Salad

1½ cups diced cooked chicken or turkey breast
1½ cups diced cooked beets
1½ cups diced Gruyère cheese
2 medium potatoes, boiled, drained and diced
2 small green bell peppers, cored, seeded and diced
small head of romaine lettuce
6 tablespoons vinaigrette dressing

For garnish
1 mild or Bermuda onion, thinly sliced
2 hard-cooked eggs, sliced
1 tablespoon chopped chives

Method
Mix the chicken or turkey breast, beets, cheese, potatoes and peppers with the vinaigrette dressing, cover and let stand 1–2 hours.

Divide the lettuce into leaves and arrange them around a salad bowl. Pile the chicken or turkey mixture in the center, decorate with onion and hard-cooked egg slices and sprinkle the top with chives.

Note: recipes for salad dressings are on pages 32–33.

Chicken and Avocado Salad

3½–4 lb roasting chicken
2 avocados
1 carrot, peeled
1 onion, peeled
bouquet garni
1 teaspoon salt
6 peppercorns
1 celery heart
1 cup walnut halves
1½ cups boiled dressing or mayonnaise
¼ cup vinaigrette dressing
1 tablespoon chopped mixed herbs (parsley and chives)
1 teaspoon chopped gherkin pickles

Method
Put chicken in a kettle and cover with water. Add carrot, onion, bouquet garni and seasonings, cover and simmer gently for 45–55 minutes or until tender. Leave to cool in the liquid.

Wash and trim celery heart and cut into julienne strips; soak in ice water for 1 hour, then drain and dry on paper towels. Drain chicken, discard the skin and bones, and cut the meat into small neat pieces. Mix with celery and walnuts, pour on boiled dressing or mayonnaise and toss to coat well. Spoon salad onto a serving dish.

Peel and quarter avocados and remove seeds; arrange around chicken salad. Mix vinaigrette dressing with herbs and pickles, and spoon over avocados immediately to prevent them from browning. Serve as soon as possible.

French roast chicken with cherries in tarragon cream dressing

Chicken and Cherry Salad

3½–4 lb roasting chicken
¼ cup butter
salt and pepper
1½ cups stock (made from the giblets)
1 lb fresh red cherries, pitted, or 1 can (1 lb) red cherries in water or light syrup, drained
1 cup tarragon cream dressing
2 Bibb or firm Boston lettuce

For vinaigrette dressing
1 tablespoon wine vinegar
¼ cup oil
1 tablespoon mixed chopped herbs (parsley, mint, thyme)

Trussing needle and string

Method
Set oven at hot (400°F).

To 'French roast' a chicken: rub inside of chicken with 1 tablespoon butter and season with salt and pepper. Spread remaining butter over outside of bird, truss it, cover with foil or buttered brown paper and pour over half the stock. Roast in heated oven for 1¼ hours, or until juice is no longer pink when the thigh is pierced. Baste bird and turn it from time to time during cooking so it browns evenly. Remove foil or paper for the last few minutes of roasting to complete browning. When cooked, remove chicken from the pan, discard the fat, pour in remaining stock, boil it well to dissolve the pan juices, strain and reserve.

Carve chicken in pieces and arrange on a platter. Mix vinegar with salt and pepper and whisk in the oil. Add juices and herbs to the oil and vinegar mixture. Taste dressing for seasoning and spoon it over the chicken.

Mix cherries with the tarragon cream dressing. Wash lettuce, remove outer leaves and cut hearts in two. Fill with the cherry mixture and place on the platter with the chicken.

Green Goddess Salad

1 lb peeled, cooked shrimps, crab meat, or chicken
1 head of romaine lettuce

For Green Goddess dressing
4 anchovy fillets, finely chopped
1 scallion white part, finely chopped
2 tablespoons chopped parsley
2 tablespoons chopped chives
1 tablespoon chopped tarragon
$\frac{1}{2}$ clove of garlic, crushed
$\frac{1}{2}$ cup sour cream
$\frac{1}{2}$ cup mayonnaise
2 tablespoons tarragon vinegar
2–4 tablespoons heavy cream
salt and pepper

Green Goddess dressing was created in 1915 at the Palace Hotel, San Francisco, in honor of George Arliss, who was starring in a play entitled 'The Green Goddess'.

Method
To make Green Goddess dressing: in a bowl mix the anchovy fillets, scallion, parsley, chives, tarragon and garlic. Add the sour cream and mayonnaise, stir in the tarragon vinegar and enough heavy cream to make a dressing that pours easily. Taste for seasoning.

Tear the lettuce into bite-sized pieces and toss with half the dressing. Spread the lettuce on 4 individual plates, pile the shrimps, crab meat or chicken on top and serve the remaining dressing separately.

Jellied Tongue Salad

$\frac{3}{4}$ lb cooked tongue, cut in thick julienne strips
1 can consommé
$\frac{1}{4}$ cup sherry
$\frac{1}{2}$ envelope gelatin
2 tablespoons water

For potato salad
10–12 small new potatoes
$\frac{1}{4}$ cup white wine
salt and pepper
bunch of radishes
2 tablespoons heavy cream

For orange dressing
grated rind and juice of 1 orange
salt and pepper
2 teaspoons wine vinegar
$\frac{1}{2}$ cup olive oil

For garnish
bunch of watercress

Ring mold (1 quart capacity)

Method
Heat consommé and add the sherry. Sprinkle gelatin over the water and stand 5 minutes until spongy; stir into the hot consommé until dissolved; cool.

Put shredded tongue in the wet mold and, when consommé is quite cold but still liquid, spoon it in to fill the mold. Chill for 2 hours or until set.

Scrub or peel potatoes and cook in boiling salted water for 15–20 minutes or until just tender. Drain, leave whole and, while still hot, sprinkle with the white wine, salt and pepper. Wash and trim radishes, soak in ice water for 10–15 minutes, then drain and slice finely. Combine the potatoes and radishes, add cream and spoon into a serving dish.

Mix the grated orange rind with seasoning, vinegar and strained orange juice. Whisk in the olive oil until the dressing is smooth and emulsified, taste for seasoning and pour into a sauce boat or bowl.

Just before serving, unmold the jellied tongue onto a platter and fill the center with watercress. Serve the orange dressing and potato salad separately.

Fruit Salad Platter

2 heads of Bibb lettuce
$\frac{1}{2}$ fresh pineapple or 4 rings canned pineapple, drained
2 oranges
1 grapefruit
2 tomatoes, peeled and sliced
$1\frac{1}{2}$ tablespoons chopped chives
2 tablespoons heavy cream
1 cup (8 oz) cottage cheese
salt
2 dessert pears
2 peaches
juice of $\frac{1}{2}$ lemon
2 teaspoons chopped mint

Method
Wash and dry the lettuce well, wrap in a cloth or paper towels and leave in refrigerator to crisp.

If using fresh pineapple, cut away skin, cut the fruit in four slices and remove the core with a small cutter or apple corer. Peel oranges and grapefruit, divide into sections and remove all the membranes. Stir the chives and cream into the cottage cheese and add salt.

Arrange a bed of lettuce on four plates, place a ring of pineapple in the center of each one; spoon cheese mixture on top. Place prepared oranges, grapefruit and tomatoes around.

Pare the pears; scald the peaches and peel them. Cut both fruits in half and remove the cores and pits. Mix lemon juice with the mint and spoon the mixture carefully over the pears and peaches. Place a pear and peach half on each plate and serve as soon as possible, before the fruit begins to discolor.

Royal Salad

$\frac{1}{2}$ fresh pineapple
3 oranges
3 dessert apples
small head of celery, sliced
1 cup mayonnaise
3–4 tablespoons heavy cream

For garnish
1 green bell pepper, cored, seeded and chopped
1 red bell pepper, cored, seeded and chopped, or 2 slices of canned pimiento, drained and chopped
$\frac{1}{4}$ cup chopped pecans

Method
Cut away the pineapple skin, and cut in chunks, discarding the core. Peel the oranges, divide into sections and remove all the membranes. Wipe the apples, core and dice them, but do not pare. Mix the fruit with the sliced celery.

Stir enough cream into the mayonnaise so it pours easily and mix it with the fruit.

Pile the salad on a platter and arrange small piles or 'bouquets' of chopped green and red peppers around the edge. Sprinkle the top with chopped pecans.

Note: recipes for salad dressings are on pages 32–33.

Salad Dressings

A dressing marries the ingredients of a salad and complements the other flavors without destroying their individuality. Use herbs and spices with discrimination and add wine or cider vinegar rather than the harsh, distilled kind. Oil is a matter of personal choice — olive oil is good with robust vegetables like cabbage and with cooked meats, but you may prefer a lighter peanut or vegetable oil.

Always taste a salad before serving, because bland ingredients like lettuce absorb a good deal of salt and pepper and more may be needed than when the dressing was tasted alone.

Vinaigrette Dressing

For $\frac{1}{2}$ cup: mix 2 tablespoons cider, tarragon or red or white wine vinegar with $\frac{1}{2}$ teaspoon salt and $\frac{1}{2}$ teaspoon freshly ground black pepper. Gradually add 6 tablespoons olive or peanut oil, whisking until the dressing thickens slightly. Taste for seasoning. Chopped fresh herbs (thyme, marjoram, basil or parsley) are an excellent addition, as is a pinch of sugar.

Mayonnaise

2 egg yolks
salt and pepper
pinch of dry mustard
$\frac{3}{4}$ cup oil
2 tablespoons wine vinegar

Makes about 1 cup.

Method

Beat egg yolks and seasonings until thick in a bowl with a small whisk or wooden spoon, or use an electric mixer. Add the oil drop by drop, beating constantly. When 2 tablespoons of oil have been added, mixture should be very thick. Stir in 1 teaspoon of vinegar.

The remaining oil can be added a little more quickly, either 1 tablespoon at a time and beaten thoroughly between each addition until it is absorbed, or in a thin steady stream if using an electric mixer.

When all the oil has been incorporated, add remaining vinegar to taste, with extra salt and pepper as necessary.

To thin and lighten mayonnaise, add a little hot water. For a coating consistency, thin with cream or milk.

Watchpoint: mayonnaise curdles easily and it is important to remember the following points.

1 Eggs should be at room temperature, not chilled.

2 If oil is cold or appears cloudy, warm it slightly over a pan of hot water.

3 Add the oil drop by drop at first and continue adding it very slowly. If the mayonnaise will no longer thicken or starts to separate, stop adding oil and beat well. If mayonnaise has separated slightly, try beating in a tablespoon of boiling water.

4 If mayonnaise curdles, start with a fresh yolk in another bowl. Beat well with seasoning then add the curdled mixture to it very slowly and carefully, as for the oil. When the curdled mixture is completely added, more oil can be beaten in if the mixture is too thin.

Blender Mayonnaise

2 egg yolks
salt and pepper
pinch of dry mustard
$\frac{3}{4}$ cup oil
2 tablespoons wine vinegar

Makes about 1 cup.

Method
In a blender, combine egg yolks and seasonings on low speed for 30 seconds or until the mixture thickens slightly. Add the oil drop by drop, increasing the blender speed as mixture thickens. When very thick, add 1 teaspoon of vinegar and continue blending, adding the oil in a slow, steady stream. When all the oil has been added and mayonnaise is thick, add remaining vinegar to taste; thin with a little hot water or cream.

Tomato Mayonnaise

To $1\frac{1}{2}$ cups mayonnaise add 1 tablespoon tomato paste or to taste so the mayonnaise is well colored and flavored.

Green Mayonnaise

Into $1\frac{1}{2}$ cups mayonnaise stir 2 tablespoons finely chopped parsley, 1 tablespoon finely chopped chives, 1 tablespoon finely chopped tarragon and 1 teaspoon finely chopped dill.

Alternatively, purée the herbs with the mayonnaise in a blender.

Cover the mayonnaise and let stand in a cool place at least 2 hours for the flavor to mellow before serving.

Tarragon Cream Dressing

1 egg
$\frac{1}{4}$ cup sugar
3 tablespoons tarragon vinegar
salt and pepper
$\frac{3}{4}$ cup heavy cream

This dressing can be made in large quantities without the cream and, when cold, stored covered in the refrigerator. It will keep 2–3 weeks. When needed, take out the required amount and add cream. Makes about 1 cup.

Method
In a small bowl, beat egg with a fork until broken up. Add sugar and gradually beat in vinegar. Stand bowl in a pan of boiling water (or use a double boiler for the whole operation) and stir mixture until it starts to thicken. Take from the heat and stir $\frac{1}{2}$ minute longer. Season lightly and cool.

Whip cream until it holds a soft shape; fold into the cool dressing.

Note: some of these recipes have been given in previous Volumes, but are repeated here for easy reference.

Lemon Cream Dressing

grated rind and juice of
  1 lemon
$\frac{1}{2}$ cup heavy cream
$\frac{1}{2}$ cup mayonnaise
salt and pepper
$\frac{1}{2}$ teaspoon prepared mustard,
  or to taste

Serve this dressing with cooked vegetables, chicken and veal. Makes about 1 cup.

Method
Whip cream until it holds a soft shape and fold into the mayonnaise. Gradually stir in lemon rind and juice, season well and add mustard to taste. Add 1 tablespoon boiling water, if necessary, as dressing should be fairly thin. If you like, make with less cream and more mayonnaise.

Boiled Dressing

1 tablespoon sugar
2 teaspoons flour
1 teaspoon salt
2 teaspoons prepared mustard
1 tablespoon water
$\frac{1}{2}$ cup each vinegar and water,
  mixed
1 egg
1 tablespoon butter, softened
2–3 tablespoons light cream,
  or milk

This dressing can be kept covered in the refrigerator for a few days. Makes about $1\frac{1}{2}$ cups.

Method
Mix dry ingredients, add mustard and 1 tablespoon water. Stir into vinegar and water, bring to a boil, stirring, and simmer 5 minutes. Beat egg with butter, pour on hot vinegar mixture and beat thoroughly. Cook over very low heat, stirring constantly, until the dressing thickens slightly. Cool. Thin with cream or milk and mix well.

Thousand Island Dressing

1 cup mayonnaise
1 tomato, peeled, seeded and
  chopped
1 tablespoon chili sauce
1 slice of canned pimiento,
  drained and chopped
1 teaspoon chopped chives
dash of Worcestershire sauce
salt and pepper

Serve with vegetables and eggs. Makes about 1 cup.

Method
Combine all ingredients and season to taste.

PACK A FAMILY PICNIC

Here's a picnic to please all tastes — cold kebabs for sophisticates, ham and pork loaf and potato salad for traditionalists, and sticky ginger cake or grape kuchen for the sweet tooth; or make a creamy ricotta pie.

For an afternoon outdoors, there is no more appropriate wine than an informal Beaujolais. This famous district of southern Burgundy produces an ocean of good red wine, the best of which is sold under village names like Brouilly, Fleurie and Moulin-à-Vent. Beaujolais requires no aging or special handling; indeed the younger the vintage, the better it is. The gamay grape used in making Beaujolais is also raised in California and yields a less exciting but entirely pleasant red.

Picnic Choice

Herb Tomato Soup

**Picnic Loaf   Glazed Ham & Pork Loaf
Stuffed French Bread with Omelet
Deviled Turkey Kebabs
Sweet Sour Spareribs**

**German Potato Salad
Three Bean Salad**

**Concord Grape Kuchen
Sticky Ginger Cake   Ricotta Pie**

∾

*Red wine — Beaujolais (Burgundy)
or Gamay (California)*

TIMETABLE

Day before

Make soup: simmer vegetables with stock, sieve and cool. Cover and refrigerate.
Make lemonade and chill.
Make picnic loaf, wrap in foil and refrigerate.
Make and bake pie shell for ricotta pie, and store in airtight container.
Make and cook ham and pork loaf; chill, then wrap in foil to carry.
Parboil the spareribs and store them in the refrigerator.
If using fresh beans for salad, cook and drain them; if using canned, drain them. Combine beans and refrigerate.
Make dressing for three bean salad; store in airtight container.
Make and bake kuchen. Cool and cut into squares, leaving in pan. Wrap in foil and refrigerate.
Make and bake ginger cake; cool in pan, turn out and store in airtight container.

Morning

Begin preparations at 11 a.m. for departure at 1 p.m.

Unless otherwise stated, each recipe for this picnic will serve **4–6 people,** depending on appetites, and the whole menu is enough for 15–18 **people.**

Order of Work

11:00

If using oven for spareribs, bake them, let cool and wrap in foil to carry. If broiling on barbecue, pack with sauce in airtight container to carry.
Pack soup and lemonade in vacuum flasks.
Make filling and complete ricotta pie; wrap.
Prepare ingredients for turkey kebabs.

11:30

Boil potatoes for salad.
Put kebabs together and broil them or pack them to broil over barbecue at the picnic. If cooked, cool kebabs before packing.

11:50

Drain potatoes, make dressing and complete the salad; chill it and pack in container.
Chop vegetables for bean salad, add to beans with dressing and pack.

12:30

Hollow out French bread for stuffed loaves. Make omelets and put into loaves. Replace tops, cool, slice and wrap. Slice ginger cake and sandwich slices with cheese; reshape cake and wrap.
Pack food in baskets.

Herb Tomato Soup

$\frac{1}{4}$ cup butter
2 carrots, chopped
2 potatoes, chopped
6 large tomatoes, peeled and chopped
4 cups chicken stock
1 tablespoon tomato paste
salt and pepper
$\frac{1}{4}$ teaspoon tarragon
$\frac{1}{4}$ teaspoon marjoram
$\frac{1}{2}$ teaspoon thyme

Serves 6–8 people.

Method

Melt butter in a large kettle. Stir in carrots, potatoes and tomatoes and cook gently for about 5 minutes, stirring constantly. Add the stock, tomato paste, salt and pepper to taste and the herbs. Simmer the soup, covered, for about 1 hour, or until the vegetables are very tender. Strain, taste for seasoning and serve hot or cold. Pack in a vacuum flask to carry.

Sprinkle tarragon, marjoram and thyme on the herb tomato soup before simmering

Picnic Loaf

1 long loaf of French, or Italian, bread
3 tomatoes, peeled, seeded and chopped
4 scallions, chopped
$\frac{1}{2}$ cup black olives, pitted and chopped
$\frac{1}{2}$ cup pimiento-stuffed green olives, chopped
2 tablespoons finely chopped parsley
1 teaspoon capers, drained
1 tablespoon grated Parmesan cheese
2 tablespoons olive oil (to moisten)
lemon juice (to taste)
salt and pepper

Method

Hollow out the loaf of bread, working from both ends of the loaf so that it has a crust about $\frac{3}{4}$ inch thick. Make fine crumbs from the hollowed-out bread and mix them with tomatoes, scallions, both kinds of olives, parsley, capers, Parmesan cheese and enough oil to moisten the mixture. Mix in enough lemon juice to heighten the flavors and add salt and pepper to taste. Stuff the loaf with the crumb mixture, wrap it in foil and refrigerate overnight. Carry in foil and cut in slices to serve.

Glazed Ham and Pork Loaf

2 lb cooked ham, ground
1½ lb lean pork, ground
1 teaspoon salt
¼ teaspoon black pepper, freshly ground
2 eggs, beaten to mix
1 cup milk
1 cup dry white breadcrumbs
1½ cups brown sugar
1 tablespoon prepared mustard
½ cup cider vinegar
½ cup water

Method

Work ground ham and pork, salt and pepper, eggs, milk and crumbs thoroughly together. Shape the mixture into a loaf, place it in a shallow baking pan and bake in a moderate oven (350°F) for 1½ hours. Mix together brown sugar, mustard, vinegar and water in a saucepan and cook for about 5 minutes. When the loaf begins to brown, start basting it with the glaze and baste frequently during remaining baking time. Serve hot or cold. Wrap in foil or pack in an airtight container to carry.

Unless otherwise stated, each recipe for this picnic will serve **4–6 people,** depending on appetites, and the whole menu is enough for **15–18 people.**

Deviled Turkey Kebabs

16 pieces of cooked turkey meat
¼ cup olive oil
½ teaspoon dry mustard
1 tablespoon Worcestershire sauce
dash of Tabasco
2 tablespoons tomato ketchup
2 large green peppers, cored, seeded and cut into squares
8 small mushrooms
1 medium onion
4 bay leaves
8 slices of bacon

8 kebab skewers, preferably disposable

Method

Mix 1 teaspoon oil with the mustard, sauces and ketchup, pour over the turkey meat and leave to marinate while preparing the other ingredients.

Blanch the peppers in boiling water for 1 minute, drain and refresh.

Trim mushroom stems level with the caps, put caps into a bowl and cover with boiling water for 1 minute, then drain. This prevents the mushrooms from breaking when they are skewered.

Cut onion in quarters and divide into segments. Cut each bay leaf in half.

Cut each slice of bacon in half and stretch strips by smoothing out with the blade of a heavy knife. Wrap each piece of deviled turkey meat in a strip of bacon. Thread all the ingredients on the skewers in the following order: turkey, bay leaf, onion, pepper, mushroom, pepper, turkey.

Brush with oil and broil, turning the kebabs until the bacon is crisp on all sides. When cold, pack in foil or an airtight container to carry.

Cut the slices of bacon in half, stretch them with a knife and wrap around the deviled turkey meat

Thread the prepared ingredients for the deviled turkey kebabs on the skewers

---

Stuffed French Bread with Omelet

Choose small French loaves (1 loaf should serve 3 hungry people). Cut the top from each loaf, scoop out the centers; spread the insides very lightly with butter.

Fill each loaf with a 3-egg herb omelet (see Volume 1). Turn omelets out of the pan directly into the loaves and replace bread tops. Let omelets cool, then cut the loaves into slices for easy serving. Push them tightly together and wrap in foil to carry.

Sweet Sour Spareribs

4 lb spareribs
¾ cup dark brown sugar
½ cup cider vinegar
¼ cup soy sauce

Method

Parboil the spareribs in simmering water for 30 minutes and drain them. Cut them in 2–3 rib pieces.

Heat the sugar, vinegar and soy sauce until the sugar is dissolved.

To cook in an oven

Put the spareribs in a roasting pan, pour over the sauce and bake in a moderately hot oven (375°F), basting often, for 20–30 minutes or until the spareribs are tender and well browned.

To cook on a barbecue

Put the spareribs in the sauce, cover and let marinate at least 4 hours. Lift out the spareribs, lay them on the barbecue grill fairly far from the heat and broil, basting often with the sauce from marinating, for 10–15 minutes or until tender and well browned.

Serve hot or cold.

Finished kebabs are first brushed with oil, then broiled until the bacon is crisp and the onion, pepper and mushroom are cooked

Three Bean Salad

1 cup cooked green beans, halved
1 cup cooked kidney beans
1 cup cooked wax beans
½ cup finely sliced celery
2 scallions, finely sliced
2 tablespoons chopped sweet pickle

For dressing
¼ cup oil
2 tablespoons cider vinegar
salt and pepper
1 teaspoon dill

Method

Drain beans thoroughly and combine in a bowl with the celery, scallions and pickle. In a bowl beat the ingredients for the dressing together until smooth and pour over the bean mixture. Turn the mixture with two wooden spoons until salad and dressing are thoroughly combined and taste for seasoning. Chill and pack in an airtight container to carry.

German Potato Salad

5–6 freshly cooked potatoes, peeled and diced
6 slices of bacon, diced
2 tablespoons sugar
1 teaspoon flour
1 teaspoon salt
¼ cup vinegar
½ cup water
1 small onion, finely chopped
1 tablespoon chopped parsley

Method

Fry bacon in a skillet until almost crisp. Pour off all but 2 tablespoons of the bacon drippings. Stir in sugar, flour and salt until smooth. Mix vinegar with the water, add it to skillet and cook, stirring constantly, until dressing comes to a boil.

Add onion and parsley to dressing, mix well, then add boiled potatoes while they are still hot. Taste and add more salt if needed. Cool and pack in an airtight container to carry.

Unless otherwise stated, each recipe for this picnic will serve **4–6 people,** depending on appetites, and the whole menu is enough for **15–18 people.**

Concord Grape Kuchen

For pastry
2 cups flour
½ teaspoon salt
¼ teaspoon baking powder
2 tablespoons sugar
½ cup butter

For filling
2 lb Concord grapes
3 tablespoons flour
¾ cup sugar
1 tablespoon lemon juice
2 egg yolks
1 cup sour cream

8 inch square pan

Method

To make the pastry: sift flour, salt, baking powder and sugar together in a bowl. Work in butter with fingertips until mixture resembles crumbs. Press an even layer over the bottom of the pan and about two-thirds of the way up sides. Chill.

To make the filling: pinch off the grape skins, putting the pulp in a saucepan and skins in a bowl. Cook the pulp over a low heat for about 7 minutes. Remove from heat and work it through a sieve (this is an easy way to remove the seeds). Combine grape purée with grape skins, 3 tablespoons flour, ¾ cup sugar and lemon juice. Pour it into the prepared pastry shell and bake in a hot oven (400°F) for 15 minutes.

Mix egg yolks and sour cream together, pour over the surface of the kuchen and continue baking 25–30 minutes. Cut in squares to serve.

Ricotta Pie

For pastry
1 cup flour
½ teaspoon salt
⅓ cup shortening
3–4 tablespoons sherry

For filling
2 lb ricotta or creamed cottage cheese
1 cup confectioners' sugar
1 teaspoon vanilla
½ teaspoon salt
pinch of cinnamon
2 squares (2 oz) semisweet chocolate, grated
½ cup candied citron peel or cherries, finely chopped

9 inch pie pan

Method

To prepare pastry: sift flour and salt together in a bowl. Work in shortening with fingertips until the mixture resembles crumbs. Add sherry gradually, mixing with a fork or your fingers until pastry dough holds together. Chill.

To make the filling: beat the cheese, sugar and vanilla together until smooth. Mix in salt and cinnamon, then stir in chocolate, reserving 1 tablespoon, and citron peel, or cherries. Roll out dough on a floured board and line pie pan, trimming and fluting the edges. Bake blind in a hot oven (400°F) for 12–15 minutes, or until the pastry shell is golden brown. Remove from oven and cool. Spoon the filling into baked shell and sprinkle top with reserved chocolate. Chill before serving. Leave in pie pan to carry.

Spoon the ricotta or cottage cheese mixture into the cooked pastry shell

Sprinkle the ricotta pie with the grated chocolate and chill before serving

Sticky Ginger Cake

½ cup butter
½ cup brown sugar
2 eggs
1 cup molasses
2 cups flour
pinch of salt
1 teaspoon ground ginger
¾ cup golden raisins
½ teaspoon baking soda
2 tablespoons warm milk

To serve
sweet butter
Gouda or Swiss cheese

8 inch springform pan

Method

Set oven at moderately low (325°F).

Grease and flour the pan. Cream butter in a bowl, add sugar and beat until light and soft. Beat in the eggs, one at a time, and the molasses. Sift flour with salt and ginger and, using a metal spoon, fold them into the egg mixture with the golden raisins.

Dissolve the baking soda in the milk and carefully stir into the cake mixture. Pour the mixture into the prepared pan and bake in heated oven for about 1 hour, or until a skewer inserted into the center of the cake comes out clean.

Cool the cake in the pan, turn it out and cut into wedges. Spread these generously with sweet butter and insert a slice of Gouda or Swiss cheese. Re-shape into a cake and wrap in foil to carry. Serve with crisp dessert apples.

Picnic Drinks

There is one basic rule about drinks for a picnic — take plenty, because the hot sun and fresh air will develop great thirsts.

To make lemonade. Fresh lemonade is a welcome favorite, diluted with club soda: dissolve 2 cups sugar in 1 cup water, add the pared rind of 3 lemons, bring to a boil and simmer 5 minutes. Cool and add 1 cup lemon juice. Store in airtight container in refrigerator. When needed strain and dilute with club soda.

Don't forget the bottle opener and, if you're taking wine, a corkscrew.

Coffee. Unless you are equipped with a percolator and stove, the best way to make coffee for a picnic is to take a vacuum flask of boiling water and a jar of instant coffee. Brewed coffee tastes stewed and bitter if it is kept hot for too long in a vacuum flask.

Sauté of chicken Mâconnaise (see recipe on page 44)

HOW TO SAUTE

The word sauté can be a confusing term because it applies not only to frying briskly in a little fat but also to a type of dish, called a sauté, in which the main ingredient is fried in fat, then simmered in a small amount of liquid (usually wine or stock) until tender. Meat, poultry or game can be used, but must be young, tender and of the best quality.

A sauté usually takes its name from the sauce or any added ingredient or garnish. It is good for entertaining because it is quick to prepare and can be kept waiting without harm.

To Make a Sauté

Fry the pieces of meat lightly in oil or butter to seal in their juices. Add a small quantity of strong stock, with or without wine. The liquid should half cover the meat in the pan and is sometimes slightly thickened at this point.

When the cooking is completed, the sauce should be rich and concentrated with just enough to serve each person 2–3 tablespoons.

If possible, use the classic sauté pan that is similar to a large deep frying pan or skillet, but with straight sides and a lid. The wide base allows room for browning and for quick reduction of the liquid and the lid helps balance this reduction, if necessary, to ensure complete cooking of the meat. If you do not have a real sauté pan or a skillet with a lid, use a deep frying pan with a saucepan lid or heatproof plate as a cover.

When the meat is cooked, use your own judgment about reducing the sauce further to thicken it and strengthen the flavor.

Watchpoint: be careful not to over-reduce the sauce as this gives a harsh taste. If the flavor is right but the sauce is too thin, thicken it with a little arrowroot or cornstarch (mixed to a paste with cold water).

In some sauté recipes a sauce prepared in advance is added towards the end of cooking.

To Sauté Vegetables

Freshly boiled potatoes, especially little new ones, are delicious sautéed in butter until crisp and golden brown. Cold cooked, leftover potatoes that make very good 'pan fries' are not the same thing.

Vegetables that can be sautéed raw, with a lid on the pan, include summer squash, zucchini, eggplant, Belgian endive and small Brussels sprouts. They should be left whole or thickly sliced and cooked in butter with little or no liquid, according to the individual recipes. They don't brown, but retain all their flavor and cook comparatively quickly in 7–10 minutes.

To Cut Up a Chicken for a Sauté

For a sauté, pieces of chicken look more attractive if you cut up the bird yourself; ready-cut pieces include the backbone and won't look so neat.

Hold the chicken firmly on a board with one hand. With a sharp knife, sever the skin between the leg and breast. Then, pressing the flat of the knife against the carcass, take the leg in the other hand and bend it sharply outwards until the bone breaks away from the carcass. Slide the knife around the leg joint, cutting down towards the pope's nose, keeping it between the oyster and the backbone. The leg is now separated from the carcass and has the oyster bone (from beneath the carcass) attached. Remove the remaining leg in the same way.

Make a slantwise cut with the knife halfway up the breast across to the top of the wishbone, from the neck to the end of the wing joint. With scissors or poultry shears, cut down through the wishbone and ribs to detach the wing with a good portion of breast.

Twist the wing pinion out and tuck it under this breast meat to hold the piece flat. This makes for even browning of the meat. To obtain both wings of even size, make slantwise cuts at the same time, then detach the other wing in the same way.

Cut away the breast meat with scissors. All that is now left of the carcass are the ribs, backbone and pope's nose. If you like, the backbone can be sautéed with the five pieces of meat to add flavor, then discarded at the end of cooking.

Sauté of Chicken Mâconnaise

3–3½ lb roasting chicken
1 tablespoon oil
2 tablespoons butter
1 shallot, or scallion, finely chopped
1 cup red Burgundy
1½ cups Espagnole sauce (see Volume 2)
chopped parsley (for garnish)

For croûtes
4 slices of a small loaf of French bread
1 tablespoon oil
1–2 tablespoons butter

Method
Cut chicken into 5 pieces. Heat the oil in a sauté pan, add butter and, when foaming, put in the pieces of chicken, skin side down, in the following order.

First, the two legs and thighs because they are the thickest pieces and need the longest cooking. When beginning to brown, put in 2 wings and whole breast. Remove breast when brown.

When remaining pieces are golden brown, turn them over, return the breast to the pan with the shallot and cook gently for 2–3 minutes. This whole process should take at least 15 minutes. Pour in the wine and, when boiling, flame it to burn up the alcohol. Simmer very gently for 10–15 minutes or until the chicken is tender.

Heat the oil and butter and fry the croûtes for garnish, browning them on both sides. Drain on paper towels.

Pour the prepared Espagnole sauce onto the chicken and simmer, uncovered, for 2–3 minutes. Take out the chicken and arrange it on a hot platter. Spoon over the sauce and garnish with croûtes and parsley.

Mâconnaise denotes various meat or fish dishes flavored with red wine (a Burgundy, but not necessarily from Mâcon).

Croûtes are slices of bread cut in shapes and fried in a mixture of oil and butter until golden brown (or lightly toasted). Drain fried croûtes well on paper towels; use to garnish meat and poultry dishes.

Croûtes should not be soaked in sauce, but a corner or edge may be moistened, then dipped in chopped parsley to form a bright green border.

Sauté of chicken Mâconnaise is garnished with croûtes and sprinkled with chopped parsley

Sauté of Chicken Rajah

3–3½ lb roasting chicken, cut in 5 pieces
1 tablespoon oil
2 tablespoons butter
½ lb peeled, cooked medium shrimps

For sauce
1 cup freshly grated coconut or unsweetened flaked coconut
1 cup boiling water
2 tablespoons butter
1 tablespoon curry powder
1 tablespoon flour
salt and pepper

Method

Make coconut milk by pouring the boiling water over the coconut and leaving it to infuse for 15 minutes. Strain through cheesecloth and squeeze to extract all the 'milk'.

In a sauté pan heat the oil, add the butter and, when foaming, put in the chicken pieces, skin side down, in the following order.

First, the two legs and thighs because they are the thickest pieces and need the longest cooking. When they are beginning to brown, put in the two wing joints, then the whole breast. Turn them over and brown on the other side.

To make the sauce: melt the butter, stir in the curry powder and cook over low heat for 2 minutes; do not let it scorch. Stir in the flour and pour on the coconut milk. Bring the sauce to a boil, stirring, season and simmer 2 minutes.

When the chicken is browned, pour over the sauce, cover the pan and simmer 10–15 minutes or until the pieces are tender. Five minutes before the end of cooking, add the shrimps. Serve with mango chutney and boiled rice separately.

45

Sauté of Chicken Parmesan

2 broiling chickens (1½–2 lb each)
2 tablespoons butter
salt and pepper
juice and grated rind of ½ lemon
2–3 tablespoons stock, or water (optional)
¼ cup grated Parmesan cheese
1 egg yolk
2 tablespoons heavy cream

For béchamel sauce
2 tablespoons butter
2 tablespoons flour
1½ cups milk (infused with slice of onion, bay leaf, 6 peppercorns, blade of mace)

Method

Split chickens in half. Melt butter in a sauté pan, put in the chickens, skin side down, and cook slowly until golden brown. Turn them, season, strain on lemon juice with rind.

Cover the pan with a close-fitting lid and cook gently for 20–30 minutes or until chicken halves are tender, shaking the pan frequently to prevent them from sticking. To keep the birds moist, add a little stock or water if the pan gets dry during cooking.

Remove the birds, trim backbones, arrange on a platter and keep warm. Make béchamel sauce and stir into the pan. Boil a moment or two to dissolve the juices, then strain. Add 2 tablespoons cheese to the sauce, reheat it carefully and taste for seasoning. Combine egg yolk and cream in a bowl, and stir in a little hot sauce; add this slowly to pan, stirring. Reheat without boiling, taste for seasoning, and spoon over chicken. Sprinkle with remaining cheese and brown in a hot oven (400°F) or under the broiler.

Pork Tenderloin Normande

2–3 (about 1½ lb) pork tenderloin
2 tablespoons butter
1 medium onion, thinly sliced
1 dessert apple, pared, cored and sliced
1 tablespoon flour
½ cup cider
¾ cup stock
salt and pepper
2 tablespoons heavy cream

Method

Melt butter in a sauté pan and brown the pork tenderloins on all sides. Remove pork, add onion and cook 2–3 minutes. Add apple to the pan and continue cooking until both onion and apple are golden brown. Stir in the flour, cider and stock and bring to a boil. Replace the pork in the pan, season, cover and simmer gently for 45–50 minutes or until the meat is tender. This can be done on top of the stove or in a moderate oven (350°F).

Remove the meat from the sauce, carve it in diagonal slices and arrange on a hot platter. Strain the sauce, reheat it and stir in the cream. Taste for seasoning and spoon over the meat.

A la normande usually refers to fish dishes coated with a cream sauce (sauce Normande). When the sauce is added to small cuts of meat or chicken, it includes apples, cider and sometimes Calvados (a strong brandy made from apples). This famous apple brandy comes from the part of Normandy known as Calvados (named for the Spanish Armada ship that was wrecked on nearby cliffs in 1588).

Applejack is the American name for apple brandy and several reliable brands are on the market. There is a fiery brew made in a few country areas, not by the usual distillation method, but by freezing, so the water can be skimmed off. The potent, slightly oily liquid left is also called applejack.

The term **portugaise** usually means a tomato fondue (a concentrated purée of fresh tomatoes) made with oil and butter and flavored with onion, garlic and parsley.

However, portugaise can also refer to any garnish regarded by French chefs as prepared in the style of Portugal.

Veal Chops Portugaise

4 veal chops
1 tablespoon oil
2 tablespoons butter
1 onion, finely chopped
1 tablespoon flour
2 teaspoons tomato paste
¾ cup stock
salt and pepper
3 tomatoes
bunch of scallions
2 teaspoons chopped parsley

Method

Heat oil in a sauté pan, add the butter, then brown the chops fairly quickly on both sides. Remove from pan and add the onion. Lower heat and, after 2–3 minutes, stir in the flour. When lightly browned, blend in the tomato paste and stock. Season, add the chops, cover pan and simmer gently for 15 minutes.

Scald and peel the tomatoes, core them, remove the seeds, and cut into slices. Work the seeds in a strainer to remove all juice and add this to the sauté pan with the tomatoes. Cook 10 minutes longer or until the chops are tender.

Trim the scallions; blanch them in boiling salted water for 3 minutes, drain, refresh and add to the pan with the parsley. Taste for seasoning and serve.

Veal Cutlets Sauté Normande

4 veal cutlets
2 tablespoons oil and butter
  mixed (for frying)
1 small onion, finely chopped
1 stalk of celery, finely
  chopped
2 teaspoons flour
$\frac{1}{2}$ cup cider
$\frac{3}{4}$ cup stock
salt and pepper
2 tablespoons heavy cream

For garnish
1 Delicious or other dessert
  apple
1 tablespoon butter
2 teaspoons chopped parsley

Method

In a skillet heat the oil and butter and fry the cutlets for 2—3 minutes or until browned on both sides; sprinkle the cutlets with seasoning after turning them. Remove the cutlets and keep warm.

Add the onion and celery to the pan and fry gently until just beginning to brown. Sprinkle in the flour and cook, stirring, until lightly browned. Pour in the cider and stock, season and bring to a boil. Replace the cutlets, cover the pan and cook gently for 15 minutes or until the cutlets are very tender.

To prepare the garnish: core the apple, cut in slices without paring. Fry quickly in the butter until golden brown on both sides.

Arrange the cutlets on a platter, add the cream to the sauce, taste for seasoning and spoon over the cutlets. Arrange the apple slices, overlapping, on top and sprinkle with chopped parsley.

Veal Scaloppine à la Crème

4 veal escalopes
3 tablespoons butter
1 onion, finely chopped
$\frac{1}{3}$ cup sherry
1 tablespoon flour
$\frac{3}{4}$ cup stock
1 cup ($\frac{1}{4}$ lb) mushrooms,
  finely sliced
salt and pepper
$\frac{1}{4}$ cup heavy cream
1 cup rice, boiled (for serving)

Method

Cut the escalopes (thin pieces of meat cut from the leg or rump) in half or thirds to form scaloppine (small escalopes).

Heat a sauté pan, add butter and, while still foaming, put in the scaloppine. Cook briskly 1—2 minutes or until brown. Turn and brown on the other side; remove from pan. Add chopped onion and cook 1—2 minutes.

Pour on the sherry and boil to reduce a little. Take from the heat, stir in the flour and pour on the stock. Bring the mixture to a boil, stirring, add mushrooms and veal with salt and pepper to taste. Cover the pan and simmer gently for 8—10 minutes or until the escalopes are tender. Add the cream, taste for seasoning, bring just to a boil and serve with boiled rice.

Veal scaloppine à la crème is served with boiled rice

Sauté of Veal Marengo

1½–2 lb boneless rump or
    shoulder of veal
2 tablespoons oil
2 medium onions,
    finely chopped
1 tablespoon flour
2 teaspoons tomato paste
½ cup white wine
1½–2 cups stock
2 cloves of garlic, crushed
bouquet garni
2 tomatoes, peeled, seeded
    and coarsely chopped
salt and pepper
1 cup (¼ lb) mushrooms,
    thickly sliced

For garnish
1 teaspoon chopped parsley
triangular croûtes of fried bread

Method

Cut meat into 2 inch cubes. Heat oil in a sauté pan and brown the meat a few pieces at a time. Remove from the pan, add onions and cook slowly until golden brown, then sprinkle with the flour and continue cooking until a deep brown. Remove pan from heat, stir in the tomato paste, the wine and 1½ cups stock and blend until smooth.

Bring slowly to a boil, stirring, add the meat, crushed garlic, bouquet garni and tomatoes. Season, cover and simmer on top of the stove or cook in a moderate oven (350°F) for 45–60 minutes or until meat is tender. Stir occasionally, adding reserved stock if the sauce reduces too much.

Add the mushrooms to the pan for the last 10 minutes of cooking. Transfer the sauté to a hot deep platter, sprinkle with parsley and surround with croûtes.

Kidneys Sauté with Madeira

3–4 (about 1½ lb) veal kidneys
1 tablespoon oil
1 tablespoon butter
1 onion, chopped
1 tablespoon flour
¼ cup Madeira or port
1 cup stock
2 shallots, finely chopped
clove of garlic, crushed
bouquet garni
1 teaspoon tomato paste
salt and pepper
mashed potatoes for piping
    (see box)

Pastry bag and a star tube

Method

Skin the kidneys, if necessary, cut out and discard the cores, and thickly slice the kidneys.

In a sauté pan heat the oil and butter and fry the kidneys, a few pieces at a time, for 1–2 minutes or until browned on both sides. Remove them, add the onion and fry until soft. Stir in the flour, cook 1 minute and replace the kidneys.

Pour over the Madeira or port and flame it. Add the stock, shallots, garlic, bouquet garni, tomato paste and seasoning. Cover the pan and simmer 25–30 minutes or until the kidneys are very tender.

Put the mashed potatoes into the pastry bag fitted with a star tube and pipe a wide border of potato around a heatproof serving dish.

Before serving, bake the potatoes in a hot oven (400°F) for 10 minutes or until browned, or brown them under the broiler.

Discard the bouquet garni from the kidneys, taste the sauce for seasoning and spoon the mixture in the center of the potatoes.

To prepare a kidney: first peel off the skin and then cut ducts with scissors

Split the kidney in half lengthwise and cut out any remaining core

Mashed Potatoes for Piping

Boil the potatoes, drain and dry them well on paper towels. Mash or put them through a sieve.

Gradually beat in boiling milk, allowing 1 cup for every 4 medium potatoes, with about 2 tablespoons butter, and season to taste. The potatoes can be kept hot up to 20 minutes by pouring 2–3 tablespoons hot milk over the leveled surface in the pan and then covering with the pan lid.

Beat the potatoes again before filling into a pastry bag.

Kidneys sauté with Madeira are served with a border of browned mashed potato

Sauté of beef with port and mushrooms; serve with peas flamande

Sauté of Beef with Port and Mushrooms

1½–2 lb flank or rump steak,
    cut in 4 even-sized pieces
¾ cup port
2 cups (½ lb) mushrooms
2 tablespoons butter
1 tablespoon oil
1 tablespoon flour
1 cup beef stock
salt and pepper
2 cloves of garlic, crushed
1 tablespoon chopped parsley
    (for garnish)

Method

In a sauté pan or skillet heat 1 tablespoon butter and the oil and brown the meat on all sides. Add the port and flame; simmer until reduced by half. Transfer the meat and liquid to a bowl.

Heat the remaining butter in the pan, stir in the flour and cook until straw-colored. Add the stock and bring to a boil, stirring. Put back the meat and liquid, season, cover and simmer 1 hour.

Add the mushrooms and garlic and cook ½ hour longer or until the meat is very tender. Taste for seasoning, sprinkle with chopped parsley and serve with mashed potatoes and peas Flamande.

Peas Flamande

¾ lb scrubbed baby carrots or
    medium carrots, quartered
    and cut in 3 inch lengths
1 tablespoon butter
pinch of salt
1 teaspoon sugar
1 cup water
1 package frozen peas
black pepper, freshly ground
sprig of mint (optional)

Method

Put the carrots in a pan with half the butter, salt, sugar and water. Cover and boil 20 minutes.

Add the peas, the remaining butter and mint, if used, and continue cooking, uncovered, until all the liquid is evaporated and the carrots and peas are tender. Discard the mint and add a little black pepper just before serving.

Sauté of Haddock with Tomatoes and Mushrooms

1½–2 lb haddock fillets, cut
    in 1 inch strips
3 tomatoes, peeled, seeded
    and cut in strips
1 cup (¼ lb) mushrooms, thinly
    sliced
¼ cup butter
1 tablespoon oil
1 onion, chopped
½ cup white wine
salt and pepper
1 tablespoon chopped parsley

For béchamel sauce
2 tablespoons butter
2 tablespoons flour
1½ cups milk infused
    with 1 slice of onion, 1 bay
    leaf, 6 peppercorns, blade of
    mace

Any firm fish, such as salmon or halibut can be used for this recipe.

Method

In a sauté pan heat the oil and half the butter and fry the fish quickly, a few pieces at a time, until golden brown. Take out, add the onion and brown also.

Add the tomatoes and mushrooms, place the fish on top, pour over the wine and sprinkle with seasoning. Cover and simmer 8–10 minutes or until the fish flakes easily. Transfer fish to a platter and keep warm.

Make the béchamel sauce and add to the pan; bring to a boil, stirring. Turn down the heat, taste for seasoning and add the remaining butter in small pieces, shaking the pan so the butter is incorporated in the sauce. Do not boil or the sauce will curdle. Spoon sauce over the fish and serve with small boiled potatoes.

COOKING WITH MILK

Milk is a staple that plays an important part in the cuisine of any country that raises cattle, goats or sheep. Warm countries have storage problems so most of their milk is made into cheese or yogurt. More temperate areas use fresh milk, and their dishes are often enriched with cream and butter. Here are recipes based on milk — the different kinds of milk, cheese and cream are discussed on pages 64–65.

Cheesecake 2 (at front) and Viennese curd cake with apricot sauce – both are made with creamed cottage cheese

Cream cheese strudel is baked in a horseshoe-shape and cut in slices to serve

COOKING WITH CREAM CHEESE

Lindy's Cheesecake

For pastry
1 cup flour
$\frac{1}{4}$ cup sugar
1 teaspoon grated lemon rind
$\frac{1}{2}$ teaspoon vanilla
1 egg yolk
$\frac{1}{4}$ cup butter
1–2 tablespoons cold water

For filling
1$\frac{1}{4}$ lb cream cheese
$\frac{3}{4}$ cup sugar
1$\frac{1}{2}$ tablespoons flour
1 teaspoon grated orange rind
1 teaspoon grated lemon rind
$\frac{1}{2}$ teaspoon vanilla
3 eggs
1 egg yolk
2 tablespoons heavy cream

For glaze (optional)
1 can (8 oz) crushed pineapple
$\frac{1}{4}$ cup sugar
2 teaspoons lemon juice
1 tablespoon cornstarch
1 tablespoon water

9 inch springform pan

Serves 6–8 people.

Method
To make the pastry: sift flour into a bowl and add the sugar and lemon rind. Make a well in the center and into this put vanilla, egg yolk, butter and water. Work with the hand to form a smooth dough. Chill at least 1 hour.

Set oven at hot (400°F). Lightly oil the pan. Roll about a quarter of the dough directly onto the base of the pan and trim the edges. Bake in heated oven for 10 minutes or until golden brown; cool.

Divide remaining dough into 2 parts on a lightly floured board. Roll out each part into strips about 1$\frac{1}{2}$ inches long, one-eighth inch thick. Line strips around sides of pan to meet dough on the base, pressing the edges to make neat joins. Trim top edge of dough so it reaches three-quarters up the sides of the pan. Turn the oven up to very hot (450°F).

In a bowl soften cream cheese and beat in the sugar, flour, grated orange and lemon rind and vanilla. Add the eggs, one at a time, and egg yolk, stirring lightly after each addition. Stir in the cream.

Pour cheese filling into pastry shell and bake in heated oven for 10 minutes. Reduce heat to very low (200°F) and continue baking for 1 hour or until firm and brown.

Remove from the oven and cool. When quite cold, remove sides of pan carefully. Serve without taking off the base.

To make the glaze: in a saucepan combine pineapple, sugar and lemon juice and bring to a boil. Mix cornstarch with water until smooth and stir into the pineapple mixture. Bring to a boil, stirring, and simmer 1 minute until glaze is clear and slightly thick. Cool and spread over the top of the cheesecake.

Cream Cheese Strudel

For pastry
1$\frac{1}{2}$–2 cups flour
pinch of salt
1 small egg
2 teaspoons oil
$\frac{1}{2}$ cup warm water

For filling
1$\frac{1}{2}$ cups cream cheese
$\frac{1}{4}$ cup butter
$\frac{1}{4}$ cup sugar
$\frac{1}{2}$ cup dark or golden raisins, soaked in warm water until puffed
grated rind of 1 lemon, and juice of $\frac{1}{2}$ lemon
2 teaspoons flour
2 egg yolks or 1 egg, beaten to mix
$\frac{1}{4}$ cup melted butter
2–3 tablespoons browned breadcrumbs
confectioners' sugar (for sprinkling)

Method
To make the pastry: sift 1$\frac{1}{2}$ cups flour into a bowl with salt and make a well in the center. Beat the egg, add oil and warm water and pour into the well. Work together to make a smooth elastic dough, adding more flour if necessary so the dough is soft but not sticky.

Knead 5 minutes, cover with an inverted bowl and leave in a warm place for 10–15 minutes. Roll out the dough to $\frac{1}{4}$ inch thickness and lift onto a large floured cloth, spread out on a table. (The cloth and table should be at least 3 feet square.) Leave 7–10 minutes for the dough to lose its elasticity.

Set oven at hot (400°F).

To make the filling: cream the butter, beat in the sugar until light and fluffy and gradually beat in the cream cheese. Thoroughly drain the raisins and add to the cheese mixture with lemon rind and juice, flour and egg.

Stretch the dough very gently, pulling the edges with both hands until it is paper thin — it is easier for two people to do this. If you are alone, hold down one side with the rolling pin while pulling the other. (The dough should be so transparent that you could read a letter through it.)

Brush the dough carefully with melted butter and scatter with browned breadcrumbs. Dot with the filling and trim off all the thick edges of the dough. Roll up the strudel by tilting the cloth so the dough turns upon itself. Tip it onto a greased baking sheet, form it into a horseshoe, brush with melted butter and bake in heated oven for 30–40 minutes or until golden brown. Cool, sprinkle with confectioners' sugar, if you like, and cut into slices. Serve with a cherry compote (see Volume 3).

Strudel to us is a delicious pastry made of many thinly rolled layers spread with filling. However, in Bavaria, where it originated, noodle dough is rolled out to a paper-thin sheet and cut into squares. Each square is spread with a mixture of diced apples, butter, currants and chopped almonds and flavored with cinnamon and brandy. The squares are then rolled up, browned in butter and poached in milk in the oven. The finished strudel squares are served hot, sprinkled with sugar.

Almond Cheesecake

5 tablespoons butter
¾ cup sugar
1¼ cups cream cheese
2 eggs, separated
½ cup whole blanched almonds, ground
½ cup raisins
2 tablespoons cream of wheat
grated rind and juice of 1 lemon

9 inch springform pan

This cheesecake may be served alone or with a fruit sauce. Serves 6 people.

Method
Set oven at moderate (350°F). Line pan with a circle of wax paper.

Cream the butter, beat in sugar until light and fluffy; then gradually beat in the cream cheese. Add egg yolks one by one, beating well between each addition. When very creamy, stir in the ground almonds, raisins, cream of wheat, lemon rind and juice. Beat egg whites until they hold a stiff peak and fold into the cheese mixture. Spoon into the prepared pan and bake in heated oven for 45–55 minutes or until brown and set.

Cool a little, loosen sides of pan and cool completely before removing the base.

COOKING WITH COTTAGE CHEESE

Cheesecake 1

For pastry
1½ cups flour
½ cup butter, softened
6 tablespoons sugar
2 egg yolks
grated rind and juice of ½ lemon

For filling
2 cups small curd creamed cottage cheese
6 tablespoons butter
6 tablespoons sugar
3 eggs, separated
½ teaspoon vanilla, or grated rind of ½ lemon, or to taste

8–9 inch springform pan

Serves 6 people.

Method
Sift flour onto a board and make a well in the center. Into this put the butter, sugar, egg yolks, lemon rind and juice. Work the ingredients in the well with fingers of one hand until combined, then work in the flour with the whole hand to a smooth dough. Chill 30 minutes.

Set oven at moderately hot (375°F).

Roll out pastry dough and line only the bottom of the pan. Prick it with a fork and bake until pale golden brown in heated oven for 20–25 minutes. Cool. To make the filling: cream butter, beat in sugar, egg yolks and cottage cheese. Flavor to taste with vanilla or lemon rind. Beat the egg whites until they hold a stiff peak, fold into the cheese mixture and spoon onto the baked pastry.

Return the cheesecake to the oven, lower heat to moderate (350°F) and bake for 50–60 minutes, or until the cheese mixture is set and golden brown. Cool before removing from the pan.

Cheesecake 2

For rich pie pastry
1½ cups flour
pinch of salt
½ cup butter
1 egg yolk
2–3 tablespoons water

For filling
1 cup small curd creamed cottage cheese
¼ cup butter
¼ cup sugar
3 eggs, separated
2 tablespoons heavy cream
2 tablespoons flour
½ cup raisins

10 inch flan ring, or 9 inch pie pan with removable base

Serves 6–8 people.

Method
Make pastry dough and line flan ring or cake pan; chill. Set oven at moderately hot (375°F).

To make the filling: work cottage cheese through a sieve. Cream butter, add sugar and beat well until light and fluffy. Beat in the egg yolks, cheese, cream, flour and raisins. Beat egg whites until they hold a stiff peak and fold into the cheese mixture.

Spoon the filling into pastry shell and bake in heated oven for 40–45 minutes or until the cheesecake is brown and set. Cool in the ring or pan and then turn out.

Viennese Curd Cake

1½ cups small curd creamed cottage cheese
3 tablespoons butter
1 cup zwieback crumbs
9 tablespoons sugar
½ envelope gelatin
2 tablespoons water
½ teaspoon vanilla
3 egg whites
1 cup heavy cream, whipped until it holds a soft shape

9 inch flan ring

Serves 6 people.

Method
Butter the inside of the flan ring. Melt remaining butter and stir in the zwieback crumbs mixed with 2 tablespoons sugar. Spread half the mixture in bottom of flan ring resting on a flat platter. Beat the cottage cheese with the remaining sugar.

Sprinkle the gelatin over the water in a small pan, stand 5 minutes or until spongy and dissolve over a pan of hot water. Beat into the cottage cheese mixture and add vanilla. Whip egg whites until they hold a soft shape. Fold the lightly whipped cream and then egg whites into the cheese mixture; pour into the flan ring. Smooth the top and cover with remaining crumb mixture. Chill 2 hours or until set. Remove the flan ring and serve with apricot sauce (see page 60).

Maids of Honor

1 cup quantity of rough puff
pastry (see Volume 2)

For filling
1½ cups small curd creamed
cottage cheese
1 egg, beaten to mix
2 tablespoons melted butter
¼ cup sugar
grated rind and juice of ½ lemon

*12–18 tartlet pans (2¼ inch
each) and 3 inch cookie
cutter*

These attractive little pastries
reputedly were made by Anne
Boleyn for Henry VIII when
Anne was Maid of Honor to
Queen Catherine of Aragon.

Method
Make the pastry dough and
chill 30 minutes.

To make the filling: work
the cottage cheese through a
sieve and beat in the egg,
butter, sugar, lemon rind and
juice.

Set oven at hot (400°F).

Roll out the dough to ¼ inch
thickness, stamp out the
rounds with the cutter and
line the tartlet pans. Press the
dough into the bottoms of the
pans with your thumbs and
prick lightly with a fork. Fill
with cottage cheese mixture
and bake in heated oven for
25–30 minutes or until the
pastry is puffed and brown.

COOKING WITH BUTTERMILK

Buttermilk Soup

1 quart buttermilk
4 egg yolks
¼ cup sugar
1 teaspoon vanilla
juice of 1 lemon
½ cup heavy cream, stiffly
whipped (optional)

This Danish dish can be served either as an appetizer for
a summer lunch or as a dessert. For a dessert, add more
sugar to taste and serve with
ginger or oatmeal cookies.

Method
Beat egg yolks until light. Add
sugar and beat until mixture is
thick. Add vanilla and lemon
juice and gradually stir in the
buttermilk. Taste, adding
more sugar as you like and
chill well. Top each bowl
with a spoonful of whipped
cream if you like.

Buttermilk Biscuits

1¾ cups flour
1 teaspoon salt
2 teaspoons baking powder
1 teaspoon sugar
½ teaspoon baking soda
¼ cup butter
⅔ – ¾ cup buttermilk

2 inch cookie cutter

Method
Set oven at very hot (450°F).

Sift flour, salt, baking
powder, sugar and baking
soda together. Cut in the
butter, then rub in with the
fingertips until mixture resembles crumbs. Stir in
enough buttermilk to make a
dough that is soft but not
sticky.

Turn dough onto a floured
board and knead lightly for
30 seconds or until only just
smooth. Pat to one-third inch
thickness; cut into circles
or squares with the cookie
cutter.

Place biscuits on a baking
sheet and bake 10–12 min-
utes in heated oven or until
golden brown. Serve as soon
as possible.

Buttermilk soup can be served as an appetizer or as a dessert (recipe is on page 57)

MORE MILK RECIPES

Sour Cream Cake

2¾ cups cake flour
3 teaspoons baking powder
1 teaspoon baking soda
¾ teaspoon salt
¾ cup butter
1 teaspoon vanilla
1½ cups sugar
4 egg whites
1 cup sour cream
½ cup milk

Three 8 inch cake pans

Method

Set oven at moderate (350°F). Grease and flour cake pans.

Sift the flour, baking powder, soda and salt together several times. Cream butter with vanilla, add 1 cup of sugar and continue beating until mixture is light and fluffy. Beat egg whites until they hold a soft peak and gradually beat in remaining ½ cup sugar until this meringue is smooth and stiff.

Mix sour cream and milk together. Fold the sifted flour mixture in three portions alternately with the milk and sour cream into the creamed butter and sugar. Then fold in the meringue and pour into prepared cake pans. Bake in heated oven for 25 minutes or until the cake springs back when pressed lightly with a fingertip. Cool 5 minutes; turn out onto a wire rack. Cool completely, then sandwich and coat the cake with rich chocolate frosting.

Rich Chocolate Frosting

3 squares (3 oz) unsweetened chocolate
1¾ cups confectioners' sugar
3 tablespoons hot water, or
  1½ tablespoons rum or brandy mixed with 1½ tablespoons hot water
3 egg yolks
¼ cup butter, softened

Method

Melt chocolate in a bowl over a pan of hot water. Take from the heat and stir in sifted confectioners' sugar and hot water (or rum or brandy and water) until smooth. Beat in egg yolks, one at a time, beating hard after each addition. Beat in butter, a tablespoon at a time. Use at once.

Whipped Cream Biscuits

2 cups flour
3 teaspoons baking powder
¾ teaspoon salt
1 cup heavy cream, stiffly whipped

2 inch cookie cutter

Method

Set oven at hot (425°F).

Sift together flour, baking powder and salt and stir in the stiffly whipped cream. Turn out dough onto a floured board; knead lightly for 30 seconds or until only just smooth. Pat dough to one-third inch thickness, prick with a fork and cut into 2 inch circles, or into triangles. Put these on a baking sheet; bake in heated oven for 10–12 minutes or until golden brown, and serve as soon as possible.

Syllabub

¾ cup sugar
grated rind and juice of 2 lemons
½ cup sherry
¼ cup brandy
¼ teaspoon ground cinnamon
1½ cups heavy cream
ground cinnamon (for sprinkling)

Syllabub is an old English dessert popular in the Elizabethan era. It is usually made by beating together cream and fruit juice or wine, but at least one old recipe calls for milking a cow straight into the wine.

The name comes from Sille, a district in Champagne where the wine for syllabub came from (sparkling Champagne had not been invented in those days) and bub, Elizabethan slang for a bubbling drink.

Method

Mix the sugar with the lemon juice and heat until the sugar is dissolved. Let cool and add the sherry, brandy, lemon rind and cinnamon. Stir in the cream and beat, skimming the froth as it rises and transferring it to stemmed serving glasses.

Continue beating and skimming until all the froth has risen and only a little thin liquid remains. If you like, pour this liquid into the glasses — it will fall to the bottom to form a separate layer.

Chill the syllabub for 4–6 hours before serving with ladyfingers. Sprinkle the top of each with a little ground cinnamon before serving.

MILK PUDDINGS

Milk puddings are easy to make and delicious when they are baked in a low oven until soft and creamy. A variety of cereals can be used – rice, barley or rolled oats – and cream may be added for richness.

Oatmeal Cream

2 cups milk
½ cup rolled oats
1 large egg, beaten to mix
grated rind and juice of ½ lemon
1–2 tablespoons sugar
    (or to taste)
½ envelope gelatin
2 tablespoons water
½ cup heavy cream, whipped
    until it holds a soft shape
fruit sauce – apricot, raspberry,
    etc. (to serve)

Method
Soak rolled oats in the milk for 30 minutes, pour into a saucepan, place over moderate heat and stir until boiling. Simmer 3–4 minutes, pour mixture into a bowl and stir in beaten egg, lemon rind and sugar. Cool.

Sprinkle gelatin over lemon juice and water in a small pan and let stand 5 minutes or until spongy. Dissolve over a pan of hot water and stir into the cooled oatmeal mixture. Fold the lightly whipped cream into the oatmeal mixture. Pour into a glass bowl and chill until set. Spoon 3–4 tablespoons of the chosen fruit sauce over top before serving.

Rice Cream

¼ cup round grain rice
2½ cups milk, or half and half
sugar (to taste)
½ cup heavy cream, whipped
    until it holds a soft shape

This dessert can be cooked in a double boiler, but it will not be as creamy because evaporation will be less.

Method
Wash the rice, put it in a saucepan with the milk or half and half, bring slowly to a boil and simmer 35–40 minutes or until the rice is tender, stirring occasionally to prevent it from sticking.

If the mixture gets too thick, add a little more milk or half and half.

Pour the rice mixture – it should pour easily – into a bowl, sprinkle with sugar and cool.

When the rice is cold, gently fold in the lightly whipped cream. Taste, add more sugar if you like, and spoon the cream into a serving dish.

Cold Apricot Sauce

Simmer ¾ cup (¼ lb) dried apricots in 1½ cups water with a strip of lemon rind for 15 minutes or until tender. Remove lemon and work mixture through a sieve or purée in a blender. Add sugar to taste and thin with a little water, if necessary.

Hot Apricot Sauce

In a saucepan heat 1½ cups (12 oz jar) apricot jam with ½ cup water and the juice of 1 lemon. When jam is melted, strain the sauce, return to pan and reheat. Add more lemon juice or sugar to taste.

Rice Cream Tyrolhof

¼ cup rice
2½ cups milk
¼ cup sugar
1 large dessert apple
1 envelope gelatin
3 tablespoons orange juice,
    or water
¼ cup heavy cream, stiffly
    whipped
cold apricot sauce (for serving)
2 tablespoons slivered
    almonds, browned

For decoration
½ cup heavy cream, stiffly
    whipped

*Ring mold (1 quart capacity);
pastry bag and medium star
tube*

Method
Lightly oil the mold. In a pan, simmer the rice in the milk for 35–40 minutes or until tender and creamy, stirring occasionally. Take from heat, stir in the sugar and cool. The consistency should be thick, but not solid. Add a little more milk if necessary.

Sprinkle gelatin over orange juice or water in a small pan and stand 5 minutes or until spongy. Stir into the hot rice until dissolved, then let rice cool.

Pare, core and dice the apple and add to the rice. Fold the stiffly whipped cream into the rice cream when it just starts to set. Pour it into the prepared mold; chill 2 hours or until firmly set.

Just before serving, turn out the cream onto a deep platter. Fill the remaining stiffly whipped cream into the pastry bag fitted with the star tube and decorate the rice cream with rosettes. Scatter over the slivered almonds and spoon the apricot sauce around.

Bread and Butter Pudding

3–4 slices of white bread, well
    buttered, preferably from a
    firm loaf
¼ cup currants or raisins
½ cup golden raisins
grated rind and juice of ½ lemon
sugar (for sprinkling)

For custard
2½ cups milk, or half and half
2 eggs
1 egg yolk
1 tablespoon sugar

*Ovenproof dish (1 quart
capacity)*

Method
Set oven at moderate (350°F).

To make the custard: scald the milk; beat eggs and egg yolk with a fork to mix and stir in the sugar. Gradually pour on the scalded milk, stir thoroughly and strain.

Cut each slice of bread in 4 pieces, leaving on the crusts. Put a layer in the bottom of the buttered dish, scatter in some dried fruit and a little lemon rind and juice and then add another layer of bread. Scatter on remaining fruit and lemon and finish with a layer of bread.

Pour in the custard carefully at the side of the dish and sprinkle the top of the pudding generously with sugar. Stand the dish in a water bath and bake in heated oven for 30–40 minutes or until the custard is set creamily and the top is brown. Serve hot or cold.

Note: as a variation, make this pudding with a miniature loaf of French bread cut into about sixteen ½ slices. The final layer of circles makes an attractive pattern on top of the pudding.

Rice Pudding

2 tablespoons round grain rice
2 tablespoons cold water
2½ cups milk, or half and half
1 tablespoon butter, melted
1½ tablespoons sugar
pinch of nutmeg (optional)

Ovenproof dish (1 quart capacity)

Method

Wash rice and put in the bottom of the baking dish. Add cold water and soak 1 hour. Set oven at low (300°F).

Drain all water from the rice and pour on milk or half and half. Stir in the butter, sugar and nutmeg. Bake in heated oven for 2½–3 hours. After the first hour, or when a skin is just beginning to form, stir with a fork. Then leave without stirring until the skin is golden brown and the rice and milk are thick and creamy. If the pudding is still sloppy 30–40 minutes before serving time, raise oven temperature to moderately low (325°F). Serve hot or cold.

If serving cold, remove from oven when still slightly creamy; pudding will stiffen while cooling.

Barley Pudding

Make as for rice pudding but use 2 tablespoons barley instead of rice.

Norwegian cream is covered with whipped cream and chocolate caraque

Mecca Cream

1 cup milk
½ teaspoon vanilla, or ½ vanilla
   bean
5 tablespoons butter
7 tablespoons flour
2 large eggs
¼ cup slivered almonds
confectioners' sugar
   (for sprinkling)
hot apricot sauce (for serving)

Soufflé dish, or ovenproof dish (3 cup capacity)

Method

Thoroughly butter the dish; set oven at hot (400°F).

In a saucepan bring the milk slowly to a boil with the vanilla bean (do not add vanilla at this time). Remove the bean and add the butter. When milk is bubbling, take from the heat and pour in the flour all at once. Beat the mixture hard until it is smooth, add the vanilla, if using, and cool.

Beat in the eggs, one by one, and when the mixture looks shiny, spoon it into the prepared dish. Scatter almonds over the top and bake the cream in heated oven for 40–45 minutes, or until well risen and firm to the touch.

Sprinkle with confectioners' sugar and serve at once with hot apricot sauce.

Norwegian Cream

2 tablespoons apricot jam
3 eggs, 1 separated
1 tablespoon sugar
½ teaspoon vanilla
2 cups milk
½ cup heavy cream, stiffly
   whipped
chocolate caraque, or grated
   chocolate (to finish)

Soufflé dish (3 cup capacity)

Method

Spread apricot jam over the bottom of the soufflé dish. Set oven at moderate (350°F).

In a bowl beat 2 whole eggs, 1 egg yolk, sugar and the vanilla until creamy. Scald the milk, stir into the egg mixture gradually and strain into the soufflé dish.

Stand the dish in a water bath, cover with foil or silicone paper, tie around with string, and bake in heated oven for 45–50 minutes, or until a knife inserted near the center comes out clean.

Chill. Whip remaining egg white until it holds a stiff peak. Fold with the stiffly whipped cream. Cover the cold custard with a layer of chocolate caraque or grated chocolate, pile the cream and egg white mixture on top and decorate with more caraque.

Chocolate Caraque

Melt 3 squares (3 oz) semi-sweet chocolate on a heatproof plate over a pan of hot water. Work with a metal spatula until smooth and spread thinly on a marble slab or Formica-type surface. Leave until nearly set.

Hold a sharp, long knife almost at a right angle to the surface; shave off long chocolate scrolls or flakes using a slight sideways sawing movement. Caraque looks better when fresh but can be kept a day or two in an airtight tin.

Milk drinks are (from left): iced coffee shake, eggnog 2 and a refreshing cold milk punch

MILK DRINKS

Iced Coffee Shake

This version of iced coffee is a favorite with children.

To serve 1 person: beat 1½ teaspoons instant coffee into 1 cup very cold milk and add sugar to taste. Whisk in a little whipped cream or coffee ice cream and chill until needed.

Mocha Shake

To serve 2 people: in a blender put 1½ squares (1½ oz) unsweetened chocolate, cut into pieces. Blend 5 seconds at high speed. Add ¼ cup boiling water and blend until smooth. Add 2 teaspoons instant coffee, 1½ cups cold milk and 3 tablespoons sugar or to taste. Blend until very smooth, increasing speed towards the end. Chill thoroughly. Just before serving, pour into tall glasses and top with vanilla, chocolate or coffee ice cream.

Chocolate Shake

To serve 2 people: in a blender put 1½ squares (1½ oz) unsweetened chocolate, cut into pieces. Blend 5 seconds at high speed. Add 2 cups scalded milk with ¼ cup sugar, or to taste. Blend until very smooth, increasing speed towards the end. Top with whipped cream; serve hot or cold.

Raspberry Shake

To serve 3 people: in a blender combine 1 package frozen raspberries with 3 cups milk and blend until very smooth. Strain to remove the seeds and chill thoroughly. Serve in tall glasses topped with a scoop of raspberry sherbet.

Banana Flip

To serve 2 people: in a blender put 1½ cups milk, 1 large banana, cut into pieces, 1 tablespoon honey, 2 very thin strips orange rind and 1 tablespoon rum (optional). Blend at high speed until very smooth. Chill thoroughly and serve in tall glasses, garnished with a slice of orange and a sprig of mint.

Apricot or Peach Flip

½ cup cooked apricots, pitted, or 1 large ripe peach, halved and pitted
1 cup milk
½ cup cracked ice
1–2 drops of almond extract
2 sprigs of mint (for garnish)

Serves 2 people.

Method
In a blender combine the milk, apricots or peach, the cracked ice and almond extract. Blend together at high speed until very smooth. Pour into small tumblers and decorate each with a sprig of mint.

Cold Milk Punch

2½ cups milk
2–3 strips of orange or lemon rind
5–7 tablespoons brandy, bourbon, or Scotch
2 teaspoons sugar
cracked ice

Make this in a cocktail shaker or glass jar with a tight-fitting lid. Serves 2 people.

Method
Soak orange or lemon rind in the liquor for 1–2 hours. Pour into the shaker with milk and sugar. Add a little cracked ice, shake well. Strain into glasses.

Eggnog 1

1 egg
2 teaspoons sugar
½ teaspoon vanilla, or 1½ tablespoons sherry
1 cup cold milk
pinch of grated nutmeg

There are many versions of this popular drink. This one serves 1 person.

Method
Beat egg until smooth. Gradually beat in the sugar and vanilla or sherry. Slowly beat in the milk. Strain the eggnog into a tall glass and sprinkle a little nutmeg on top. Serve very cold.

Eggnog 2

1 egg, separated
1 tablespoon sugar
2 tablespoons brandy or rum
¾ cup milk
2 tablespoons heavy cream, stiffly whipped
pinch of grated nutmeg

This is a richer eggnog recipe. Serves 1 person.

Method
Beat egg yolk with the sugar until thick and light. Add brandy or rum and beat well. Gradually stir in milk. Whip the egg white until it holds a stiff peak. Beat the whipped cream into the eggnog and fold in egg white. Pour into a glass, sprinkle with grated nutmeg and serve cold.

MANY FORMS OF

There's more to milk than you might think. A dozen or more types of milk and milk products are widely distributed throughout the country and are vital ingredients in hundreds of everyday dishes.

Fresh whole milk is available pasteurized, homogenized and fortified. Pasteurization of milk is the process of heating milk to a point where harmful bacteria are destroyed. Over 90% of all milk on the market is pasteurized; most large cities do not permit the sale of unpasteurized milk.

Homogenized milk is pasteurized milk in which the fat particles have been broken up and distributed evenly throughout the milk by a mechanical process — the result is no cream on top.

Fortified milk is pasteurized milk to which additional nutrients have been added, the most common being vitamin D.

Whole milk is also available as **canned evaporated milk.** This is homogenized milk with vitamin D added and about 60% of the water removed by heating. When diluted with an equal amount of water, it is often used in cooking. The food value remains the same as in whole fresh milk.

Canned condensed milk is made by evaporating a mixture of whole fresh milk and sugar. It differs from evaporated milk only in the addition of sugar and its extremely thick consistency. This milk is used in certain desserts, like a true Key lime pie.

Skim milk is fresh milk with most of the butterfat removed and is generally used in low-fat diets.

Buttermilk, as its name implies, is the liquid left after the butter is churned. Commercial buttermilk is usually made of skim milk to which a lactic acid culture has been added. In some parts of the country, buttermilk from neighboring farms is available. This type is usually made from whole milk and contains tiny globules of butterfat.

Dry milk, a relatively recent dairy product, has almost all the water removed during processing. Most dry milk is the instand kind that dissolves almost immediately when

MILK

mixed with water. It contains the same nutrients as milk except for fat content, and vitamins A and D. This most economical form of milk is very handy to have on the kitchen shelf. When mixed with the proper amount of water, it can be used as a drink and in cooking.

Cream, an essential ingredient in most fine cooking, is the rich, fatty part of whole milk. Classified according to its butterfat content, it can be sweet or sour but is always smooth and rich. 'Light' or 'coffee' cream has 18–20% butterfat and 'heavy' or 'whipping' cream 35–40%.

Do not try to whip light cream – it will not thicken because the butterfat content is too low.

Sour cream, also known as dairy sour cream, is made commercially from sweet cream to which a dairy culture is added for souring. Do not substitute home-soured cream in recipes calling for sour cream, because the degree of acidity or sourness cannot be controlled in your own kitchen, whereas in the commercial product it is always constant.

Half and half is another product relatively new to the dairy world; it is usually half milk and half cream – very useful in dishes where great richness isn't necessary or even desirable.

Yogurt (also spelled yoghurt), a semi-solid milk product that originated in the Balkans and Near East, is made acid (tart) by the addition of bacterial cultures. It can be made from any kind of milk, but cow's milk is commonly used in this country. The standard yogurt is plain without salt, and is an interesting ingredient in cooking. Flavored yogurt – strawberry, coffee, vanilla, blueberry, etc. – makes a refreshing dessert.

Cream cheese is made from a combination of cream and milk. It is pure white in color, spreads easily and has a flavor with a slightly acid tang.

Cottage cheese is a soft, uncured cheese made from skim milk. These days most cottage cheese is made commercially and it is mixed with a little cream to give flavor and smoothness. Federal standards require that creamed cottage cheese contain at least 4% butterfat. It is usually available in two curd sizes (indicated on the container): large curd (country or California-style) and small curd or 'old-fashioned'.

Slices of rolled lamb, filled with a savory stuffing, are garnished with watercress. Mint-flavored sauce is served in a sauce boat

MAKE YOUR MENU INTERNATIONAL

For this sole with a Spanish touch, something more than a white wine is in order. Portugal makes a host of very popular rosés, some of the best coming from the Dão district. If the Portuguese pinks are a little sweet for your taste, try a Grenache Rosé from California. With lamb, one usually thinks of a red Bordeaux, but on this occasion a wine from the Iberian Peninsula seems appropriate, and there is none finer than that from the Rioja valley. The wine is made from Bordeaux grapes in the style of the great clarets, but nonetheless has Spanish character. Equally interesting is the new Chelois wine — a Finger Lake red from French-American hybrid grapes.

Sole Andalouse

Loin of Lamb Portugaise
Buttered Noodles
Zucchini aux Fines Herbes
Crème Brûlée

∾

Rosé wine — Dão (Portugal) or Grenache (California)
Red wine — Rioja (Spain) or Chelois (Finger Lakes)

TIMETABLE

Day before
Prepare crème brûlée and refrigerate until adding the caramel topping.
Make stuffing for the lamb.

Morning
Finish crème brûlée and keep in the refrigerator. Pick over and sprinkle accompanying berries with sugar.
Bone and stuff lamb and keep in the refrigerator; make a stock.
Make the lemon sauce.
Poach fish; prepare dressing; fry tomato halves.
Wipe and slice zucchini and keep covered.

Assemble equipment for final cooking from 6:00 for dinner around 8 p.m.

Order of Work

6:00
Set oven at hot (400°F).
Put lamb in oven.
Arrange the fish on a platter, spoon over the dressing, cover and chill.

6:30
Baste lamb.

6:55
Turn the lamb, remove buttered foil and baste again.

7:15
Baste lamb again.

7:30
Start cooking zucchini. When done, keep warm in the oven.
Transfer the lamb to a warm platter and keep warm; finish the lemon sauce.

7:45
Boil the noodles.
Carve the lamb; spoon over the sauce and keep warm.
Drain noodles and keep in warm water.

8:00
Serve appetizer.
Drain and toss the noodles in butter, and add the watercress to the lamb just before serving.

> You will find that **cooking times** given in the individual recipes for these dishes have sometimes been adapted in the timetable to help you when cooking and serving this menu as a party meal.

Appetizer

Sole Andalouse

4 fillets of sole
½ cup water
squeeze of lemon juice
4 tomatoes, peeled, seeded and halved
2–3 tablespoons olive oil

For dressing
½ cup lemon and tomato purée (see box, below)
6 tablespoons olive oil
2 tablespoons wine vinegar
1 tablespoon mixed chopped herbs (parsley, chives, thyme)
salt and pepper

For garnish
4 anchovy fillets (soaked in milk to remove excess salt)

Method
Fold fillets in half and place in a wide pan. Add water and a squeeze of lemon juice, cover and poach over low heat for 10 minutes or until the fish flakes easily when tested with a fork. Cool fillets in the liquid, then drain thoroughly on paper towels.

Heat 2–3 tablespoons olive oil in a skillet and fry the tomatoes very quickly for 1 minute only. Drain, arrange in a double line down the center of a serving dish and place each fillet of fish across two tomato halves.

To prepare the dressing: combine oil, vinegar, lemon and tomato purée, add chopped herbs and adjust the seasoning. Before serving, spoon dressing over the fish fillets and garnish each one with 2 drained anchovy fillets.

Arrange the fillets of sole on the lightly sautéed tomato halves, pour over the dressing and garnish them with anchovy fillets

Lemon and Tomato Purée

In a saucepan, combine 2 fresh tomatoes, cut into pieces with the seeds removed, 1–2 teaspoons tomato paste, 1 clove garlic, crushed, grated rind and juice of ½ lemon, and salt, pepper and sugar to taste, cover and cook gently for 12–15 minutes or until the tomatoes are very soft. Stir occasionally to prevent the mixture from sticking. Work the mixture through a sieve or purée in a blender and cool. If puréeing in a blender, peel the tomatoes before cooking.

Sole andalouse is garnished with strips of anchovy fillet

Entrée

Loin of Lamb Portugaise

2½—3 lb loin of lamb,
   including chine bone
3—4 tablespoons butter
½ cup white wine
bunch of watercress
   (for garnish)

For stock
4 cups water
1 small onion, quartered
1 carrot, quartered
bouquet garni
salt and pepper

For stuffing
1 cup chopped walnuts
1 medium onion, chopped
3 tablespoons butter
½ cup fresh white breadcrumbs
1 tablespoon chopped parsley
1 teaspoon marjoram
grated rind and juice of ½ lemon
1 egg, beaten to mix

For lemon sauce
juice of ½ lemon and juice of
   ½ orange
2 tablespoons butter
1½ tablespoons flour
1 tablespoon red currant jelly
1 tablespoon chopped mint

String, or small skewers

Breast of lamb is a more economical alternative to loin in this recipe.

Method
To make the stock: put the lamb bones in a pan with water, onion, carrot, bouquet garni and seasoning, cover, and simmer 45—50 minutes. Strain and boil to reduce the stock to 1½ cups.

To prepare the stuffing: grind walnuts in a food mill or in an electric blender. Cook onion in butter until it is soft and golden. Stir in the nuts mixed with breadcrumbs, herbs, lemon rind and juice, and enough beaten egg to hold the mixture together. Season well with salt and pepper.

Spread stuffing over the cut surface of the lamb, roll it neatly and secure with string or small skewers. With a sharp knife lightly score surface of lamb in a diamond pattern and spread the meat with butter. Place in a roasting pan, pour around the wine, cover with buttered foil and roast in a hot oven (400°F) for 1¼ hours, basting occasionally, or until a meat thermometer registers 160°F for medium done meat. After 40 minutes, turn lamb and remove foil.

While lamb roasts, prepare sauce: melt butter, stir in the flour until smooth and cook it over low heat until it is a rich brown color. Take pan from heat, pour on the stock, add red currant jelly and citrus juices and stir until smooth. Season with salt and pepper to taste and cook over low heat, stirring, until sauce boils; simmer 5—10 minutes.

Transfer lamb to a platter and keep warm. Spoon fat from roasting pan, strain remaining juices and sediment into the sauce and reheat it.

Carve meat and garnish with watercress. Skim the sauce, if necessary, stir in the chopped mint and taste for seasoning. Spoon a little sauce over meat to keep it moist and serve the rest separately in a sauce boat. Serve with zucchini aux fines herbes and buttered noodles.

Stir in beaten egg to bind a savory stuffing of walnuts, onion, breadcrumbs, herbs and lemon rind and juice

Accompaniments to Entrée

Buttered Noodles

½ lb package of noodles
2 tablespoons butter
salt
black pepper, freshly ground

Method
Cook noodles in plenty of boiling salted water, 2—3 quarts at least, for 8—10 minutes or until the noodles are tender but still firm (al dente). Stir gently from time to time to prevent noodles from sticking to bottom of pan. When cooked, they should look creamy and opaque and can be severed with a thumbnail (or taste one to see if done).

Watchpoint: do not overcook noodles because they become sticky and pasty. Pour at once into a colander, rinse in hot water and drain well. Rinse pan used to cook noodles and add the butter. Return noodles to the pan and toss over low heat for 1—2 minutes. Season with salt and black pepper.

Note: if the noodles must be kept hot before serving, pour about 1 cup hot water into the pan, put in drained noodles, cover and keep warm at side of stove. When ready to serve, drain off water, add butter and seasonings and toss.

Zucchini aux Fines Herbes

4—6 medium zucchini
¼ cup butter
salt and pepper
1 tablespoon chopped fresh
   mixed herbs (parsley, chives,
   basil, thyme)

Method
Wipe zucchini with a damp cloth and trim the ends. Cut into diagonal slices about ½ inch thick. Melt butter in a large skillet, add zucchini and season to taste with salt and pepper. Cover with buttered foil and a lid.

Cook zucchini over a very low heat, shaking skillet occasionally to prevent slices from sticking, for 15—18 minutes, or until tender. Add chopped herbs and transfer to a heated serving dish.

Dessert

Crème Brûlée

2 cups heavy cream
1 vanilla bean, split, or
   1 teaspoon vanilla extract
4 egg yolks
5 tablespoons sugar

Method

Set oven at moderately low (325°F). Put cream and vanilla bean – not extract – in top of a double boiler. Cover; cook over boiling water until cream reaches scalding point (a skin wrinkles over the surface). In a bowl beat egg yolks and 1 tablespoon sugar until light in color.

Remove vanilla bean from cream, or if using vanilla extract, add at this point, and pour cream into egg yolk mixture very gradually, stirring constantly. Return mixture to pan and cook over boiling water, stirring, until custard thickens enough to coat the back of a wooden spoon.

Watchpoint: the mixture should never come to a boil, or it will curdle.

Strain the custard into a shallow baking dish and bake in heated oven for 5–8 minutes or until a skin forms on top. Remove from oven and refrigerate for several hours or preferably overnight.

Heat the broiler. Sprinkle the top of the very cold crème with remaining 4 tablespoons sugar and place it under the broiler, 4 inches from the heat. At this distance the sugar has a chance to melt before it begins to brown and the result is an even coating of crisp caramel over the crème.

Watchpoint: the broiler must be very hot or the custard will bubble through the sugar

topping before it caramelizes. If this starts to happen, remove the dish at once or the custard will burn in patches. Remove crème from broiler and let stand in the refrigerator for 2–3 hours before serving. A bowl of lightly sugared strawberries or raspberries may be served separately. The fruit is a pleasant contrast to the rich crème.

Serve crème brûlée in the dish in which it was baked, with sugared berries separately

◀ Cook custard for crème brûlée in a double boiler until it is thick enough to coat the back of a wooden spoon

Meringues Chantilly — meringue shells are filled with Chantilly cream (recipe is on page 76)

Meringues

Meringue, a mixture of egg white and sugar, is thought to have been invented in the early 18th century by a Swiss pastrycook called Gasparini, who worked in the town of Mehrinyghen.

There are three distinct types of meringue used for various dessert dishes, gâteaux and pastries: suisse, italienne, and 'cuite'. For meringue suisse and meringue italienne, the egg whites are beaten until stiff before any sugar is added. Both are made with granulated sugar, but for meringue italienne the sugar is dissolved in water as a syrup and boiled to an exact temperature before beating it into the egg whites.

In meringue cuite the egg whites are beaten only to mix, then confectioners' sugar is beaten in, a spoonful at a time, until the mixture forms a stiff peak.

Meringues must be cooked in a very low oven so they dry, rather than bake, to a delicate cream color. Oven temperature is usually given as 250°F –275°F, but thermostats are inaccurate at such low temperatures and you must use your judgment — if the meringues start to brown, turn down the heat; if they do not seem to be cooking at all, increase it.

Meringue Suisse

This is the most common type of meringue and the proportion of sugar to egg white never varies — $\frac{1}{4}$ cup sugar to each egg white.

If possible for meringue suisse use a special copper bowl with a balloon whisk for beating the egg whites; the shape of the bowl and the rounded whisk make it easy to beat in as much air as possible, and contact with the copper gives the egg whites a close, smooth texture.

A copper bowl must always be cleaned immediately before use. To do this, combine 2 tablespoons salt with 1–2 tablespoons vinegar or lemon juice in the bowl and rub with a cloth until the copper surface shines. Wash with warm water and dry very thoroughly. Any trace of dampness (or grease) on whisk or bowl, or any trace of yolk in the egg whites, will prevent them from becoming really stiff.

If you have no copper bowl, use a stainless steel bowl if possible and beat whites only to a froth with a rotary or electric beater. Continue beating by hand with a balloon whisk.

Beat until the egg whites hold a stiff peak when a little of this is lifted on the whisk, it should stay in position when shaken. When overbeaten, egg whites lose their smoothness and separate slightly at the edge of the bowl — there is less risk of this happening with a balloon whisk than with a rotary or electric beater.

Meringue suisse is used for desserts like vacherin (large rounds of meringue, filled with whipped cream, fruit, chestnuts, etc.) and Mont Blanc (recipes will be given in future Volumes), or toppings for pies like lemon meringue pie (see Volume 1).

The simplest way to serve meringue suisse is to make meringue shells which may be filled with ice cream or Chantilly cream.

A small amount of **cream of tartar, or vinegar,** is used in variations of meringue Suisse and meringue cuite for certain desserts. This gives a soft, slightly sticky consistency to such dishes as Pavlova and almond meringue cake.

Meringue Topping

For meringue suisse
2 egg whites
$\frac{1}{2}$ cup sugar (plus extra for sprinkling)

This quantity is enough to cover a 6–7 inch pie.

Method
Set oven at low (300°F).

To make meringue suisse: whisk the egg whites until they hold a stiff peak. Add 2 teaspoons sugar and whisk 1 minute until the mixture is glossy. Gradually and carefully fold in the remaining sugar with a metal spoon. Pile meringue suisse on top of the pie. Sprinkle generously with extra sugar and leave 5 minutes before putting in oven.

Bake for about 30 minutes until the meringue is delicately browned and crisp on top. The inside should be white and the consistency of marshmallow — firm and easy to cut. The meringue will remain crisp for up to 12 hours in a dry place.

Meringue Italienne

Used mainly by professional pastry chefs, meringue italienne has a light, fine texture that requires exact attention because sugar is cooked with water to a syrup and boiled to a certain temperature before it is beaten into the whites. A sugar thermometer is essential for this type of meringue.

Use meringue italienne as a topping and/or filling for cakes, and in making ice cream mixtures.

Meringue Italienne

1 cup sugar
½ cup water
4 egg whites

Sugar thermometer

This quantity will cover an 8–9 inch cake.

Method
To make the sugar syrup: put sugar with water in a pan to dissolve over gentle heat. Boil quickly, without stirring, to 220°F on a sugar thermometer.

Meanwhile, beat egg whites until they hold a stiff peak and, when the syrup is ready, pour it while still hot gradually and steadily onto the egg whites, beating constantly. Continue beating until the meringue is very stiff and glossy; it will be warm, but no longer hot.

Meringue Cuite

Cuite (cooked) is a misnomer for this type of meringue as it is not cooked during preparation. Firmer than meringue Suisse, it is used mainly for meringue baskets and pastries.

The proportions are ½ cup confectioners' sugar to each egg white. It is easy to make in large quantities with an electric beater and heat is not necessary. If beating by hand, use a rotary beater and a narrow-based bowl, so that the beater catches hold of even a small quantity of egg white; put the bowl over a pan of hot water, as the heat speeds up the thickening process.

If you bake meringue baskets in a hotter oven for a shorter time than is often advised, they will be crisp on the outside and like a marshmallow inside.

Meringue Cuite

2 cups confectioners' sugar
4 egg whites
1 teaspoon vanilla

Method
Sift the confectioners' sugar through a fine sieve onto a sheet of wax paper; if beating by hand, have a pan half-full of gently simmering water ready.

Beat the egg whites with a rotary or electric beater until frothy. Beat in the confectioners' sugar, 1 teaspoon at a time and, when all has been added, beat in the vanilla. If beating by hand, set the bowl over hot water and continue beating until the mixture will hold its shape. No heat is needed if using an electric beater.

To test, lift a little of the mixture on the beater. If ready, it will form a stiff, tall peak.

Use the meringue according to the recipe.

Meringues Chantilly

For meringue suisse
4 egg whites
1 cup sugar (plus extra for sprinkling)
1 cup Chantilly cream
oil (for brushing)
flour (for sprinkling)

2 baking sheets; pastry bag and ½ inch plain tube (optional)

These are meringue shells filled with vanilla-flavored whipped cream. This quantity makes 12–16 shells or 6–8 sandwiched meringues. Unfilled shells may be stored for up to a week in an airtight container.

Method
Set oven at very low (250°F–275°F). Brush the baking sheets lightly with oil and sprinkle with flour; bang the sheets on the table to distribute the flour evenly. Alternatively, line the sheets with silicone paper, attaching it to the sheets with a little oil or the prepared meringue.

Whisk the egg whites until they hold a stiff peak. Add 4 teaspoons sugar and whisk 1 minute until the mixture is glossy. Gradually and carefully fold in remaining sugar with a metal spoon.

Fit a pastry bag with a ½ inch plain tube and fill with meringue mixture. Pipe shells onto prepared baking sheets, or shape the mixture into shells with two spoons.

Sprinkle generously with extra sugar and leave 5 minutes to let the sugar melt slightly; this gives a shiny gloss to the finished meringue.

Bake about 1 hour, switching the sheets halfway through baking so the one on top is below and meringues bake evenly. When they are firm, carefully lift them from the sheet with a sharp knife or peel them off the silicone paper.

Press the bottoms gently to form a hollow, replace on the baking sheets, hollow side up, and continue baking 20–30 minutes, or until dry and crisp. Cool on a wire rack.

The shells are hollowed so they will hold a generous amount of Chantilly cream when sandwiched together. This type of meringue should be a rich cream color, crisp in texture and slightly sticky inside.

Serve within 1–2 hours after filling with Chantilly cream.

Chantilly Cream

Chill heavy cream, bowl and beater; on a very hot day it may be necessary to stand the bowl in crushed ice and water to prevent the cream from curdling during beating.

Beat heavy cream with an electric heater at medium speed or with a rotary beater until it holds a soft shape when the beater is lifted. For every cup of cream add 3–4 teaspoons sugar, or to taste, and ½ teaspoon vanilla. Continue beating until the cream holds a stiff peak. Do not overbeat or it will curdle.

For a delicate flavor, instead of using vanilla, sweeten the cream with vanilla sugar (see box on opposite page).

Make shells of meringue by shaping mixture with spoons

Lay shells on prepared baking sheet and sprinkle with sugar

Pipe meringue through a pastry bag fitted with a plain tube

Vanilla sugar: store 1—2 vanilla beans in a jar of granulated sugar with a few seeds scraped from the bean. Use as required.

Strawberry Meringue Baskets

For meringue cuite
2 cups confectioners' sugar
4 egg whites
1 teaspoon vanilla

For filling
1 pint fresh strawberries, hulled
2—3 tablespoons red currant jelly

Baking sheet lined with silicone paper; pastry bag and star tube

Method
Set oven at low (275°F—300°F).

Make the meringue cuite.

Fill the mixture into a pastry bag fitted with a star tube and shape 6 baskets on the prepared baking sheet. Bake in heated oven for 45 minutes, or until the baskets are crisp and lightly brown — they will still be soft inside. Cool them.

To make the filling: beat the red currant jelly in a bowl with a small whisk or fork, put it into a saucepan and heat gently until clear and melted. Take from the heat, add the strawberries and stir very carefully until each berry is coated with glaze. Spoon into the baskets.

Large Meringue Basket

For a 7 inch basket to serve 6—8 people, you will need double the quantity of ingredients used in recipe for strawberry meringue baskets. Make the meringue in two batches as one large batch is difficult to handle.

Method
Set oven at low (275°F); line 2 baking sheets with silicone paper.

Make the first batch of meringue cuite and put just over half into a pastry bag fitted with a $\frac{1}{2}$ inch plain tube. Use this mixture to shape a round about 7 inches in diameter and one hoop ring of the same size. Bake both in heated oven for 45—50 minutes or until dry and crisp. Meanwhile keep the remaining meringue mixture covered with a damp cloth to prevent it from hardening in the bowl.

When the round and ring are cooked, cool them on a wire rack and peel off the paper. Turn over this paper, replace on the baking sheets and pipe two more rings, the same size as the first, with the remaining meringue. Bake and cool as before.

Make the second batch of meringue and use a little of this mixture to mount the rings on top of each other on the round. Put the remaining mixture in a pastry bag fitted with a star tube and cover the sides of the plainly piped rings with a decorative pattern. Bake again at the same temperature for 45—50 minutes until meringue is crisp.

This meringue case can be made at least a week before a party and stored in an airtight container. Fill with fresh fruit and cream or ice cream just before serving.

Above: draw a 7 inch circle on the paper to guide shaping of the base and hoop rings

Above: when cool, mount the rings on circular base, sealing with a little meringue mixture
Below: pipe a pattern onto the sides of rings, bake again; fill with fruit and cream

A large meringue basket is filled and decorated with whipped cream and whole strawberries (recipe on page 77)

Sponge Cake

¾ cup flour
pinch of salt
3 eggs
½ cup sugar

8 inch springform pan

Half fill a roasting pan with a mixture of ice and rock salt and set the chilled platter on top. Put the sponge cake on the platter and sprinkle it with kirsch, if you like. Pile ice cream on the cake, using an ice cream scoop, and pipe meringue on top in a pattern to cover both the ice cream and cake completely. Sprinkle with sugar, let stand 1 minute, then bake in heated oven for 4 minutes or until the meringue is lightly browned.

To prepare this dessert ahead: about 1 hour before serving, fill the roasting pan with ice and rock salt and chill. Pile ice cream on the cake and keep it on the platter in the freezer. Make the meringue, put it into the pastry bag and keep in the refrigerator. Just before serving, cover the ice cream with meringue and bake as above.

Method

Set oven at moderately hot (375°F). Grease cake pan and sprinkle with sugar and flour, discarding the excess.

Sift the flour and salt 3–4 times. Put eggs in a bowl and gradually beat in the sugar.

If using an electric beater, continue beating at medium speed until the mixture is thick and fluffy — this will take at least 8–10 minutes and the mixture will increase in volume and lighten in color. When dropped from the beater it will make a ribbon trail on the rest of the mixture.

If beating by hand, have a pan of boiling water ready. Beat the sugar into the eggs, then place the bowl over the pan of boiling water, off the heat, and beat for at least 5 minutes until the mixture leaves a ribbon trail. The mixing bowl should rest firmly on the pan without touching the water. Remove bowl from the pan and continue beating until the mixture is cold.

With a metal spoon, cut and fold the flour into the mixture. Pour batter into the prepared pan and bake in heated oven for 20–25 minutes until the cake is golden and the top springs back when lightly pressed with a fingertip. Turn out onto a wire rack to cool.

Baked Alaska

3 egg quantity of sponge cake, (see right)
2 tablespoons kirsch (optional)
1 quart flavored ice cream

For meringue suisse
2 egg whites
½ cup sugar
½ teaspoon vanilla
sugar (for sprinkling)

Pastry bag and a medium star tube

This famous recipe is also called omelette en surprise and omelette Norvègienne. Any flavored ice cream may be used, but chocolate, strawberry or raspberry are the best. Serves 6 people.

Method

Chill a silver or stainless steel platter thoroughly and set oven at hot (425°F).

Make the meringue and put into the pastry bag fitted with the star tube.

Baked Alaska — hard ice cream and sponge cake are covered with meringue and then baked until lightly browned

Almond Meringue Cake

1 cup whole blanched almonds,
 browned and ground (see
 box, page 106)
1 teaspoon vanilla
½ teaspoon vinegar

For meringue suisse
4 egg whites
1 cup sugar

For filling
Chantilly cream, made with
 1 cup heavy cream,
 3—4 teaspoons sugar and
 ½ teaspoon vanilla (see
 page 76)
1 pint fresh red raspberries
 or 1 package frozen red
 raspberries, thawed and
 drained
confectioners' sugar
 (for sprinkling)

*Two 8 inch cake pans; pastry
bag and a medium star tube*

Method
Line the cake pans with a
circle of wax paper, grease
them and sprinkle with flour,
discarding the excess. Set
oven at moderately hot
(375°F).

Make the meringue suisse
as for meringues Chantilly
(see page 76) and beat in the
vanilla and vinegar. Fold in
the ground almonds.

Divide the mixture between
the prepared pans and smooth
the tops. Bake in heated oven
for 30—40 minutes. The top
of the meringue will be crisp
and the inside soft like a
marshmallow (due to the
addition of vinegar). Turn the
cakes out onto a wire rack to
cool.

Spread the Chantilly cream
on one meringue round. Pile
the raspberries on top and
replace the other round.
Sprinkle the top with confectioners' sugar.

Watchpoint: layer the meringue with filling at least 3
hours before serving so the
cake softens and can be cut
into neat wedges without
crumbling.

*For Chantilly cream, beat the
cream, sugar and vanilla until
the cream holds a stiff peak*

*Spread the Chantilly cream on
one meringue round*

Blidahs

¾ cup whole blanched
 almonds, ground
grated rind of 2 oranges
red and yellow food coloring
confectioners' sugar
 (for sprinkling)
¼ cup shredded almonds

For meringue suisse
3 egg whites
¾ cup sugar

*Pastry bag and ⅜ inch plain
tube*

Makes 10—12 blidahs.

Method
Set oven at moderately low
(325°F). Brush baking sheets
with oil and sprinkle with
flour; bang the sheets on the
table to distribute the flour
evenly. Or, line baking sheets
with non-stick silicone paper.

Make the meringue suisse
as for meringues Chantilly (see
page 76). Fold in the ground
almonds and orange rind; stir
in a few drops of food coloring
to make an orange color.

Fill the mixture into a pastry
bag fitted with a plain tube
and pipe the mixture onto the
prepared baking sheets in
spirals to form ovals. Smooth
the tops of the ovals with a
metal spatula and sprinkle
generously with confec-
tioners' sugar. Top with a few
shredded almonds. Bake in
heated oven for 15—20
minutes or until browned. Let
cool slightly, then transfer
to a wire rack to cool completely.

Almond meringue cake is filled with Chantilly cream and fresh raspberries

Milk Meringue Flan

For French flan pastry
scant 1 cup flour
pinch of salt
$\frac{1}{4}$ cup butter, softened
$\frac{1}{4}$ cup sugar
2 egg yolks
$\frac{1}{2}$ teaspoon vanilla

For filling
3 eggs
$\frac{1}{2}$ cup sugar
3 tablespoons flour
$1\frac{1}{2}$ cups milk
1 teaspoon vanilla

For meringue suisse
2 egg whites
$\frac{1}{2}$ cup sugar (plus extra for
   sprinkling)
1 tablespoon red currant jelly
   (for decorating)

*8 inch flan ring; pastry bag and
a medium star tube*

Method
Make the pastry dough (see right) and chill 30 minutes. Roll out and line the flan ring; set oven at moderately hot (375°F).

To make the filling: beat the eggs with the sugar and flour until mixed; stir in the milk and vanilla. Strain this custard into the uncooked pastry shell and bake in heated oven for 25–30 minutes or until the filling is set and browned. **Watchpoint:** set the baking sheet with the flan ring on another hot baking sheet inside the oven, so the pastry cooks more quickly and is not soggy.

Turn down oven to low (300°F).

Make the meringue suisse as for meringues Chantilly (see page 76) and spread half of it in a layer on top of the filling. Put the remaining meringue into the pastry bag fitted with a star tube and decorate the top with rosettes. Sprinkle the top with sugar, leave 5 minutes, then bake the flan in the heated oven for 15–20 minutes or until the meringue is browned. Let cool, then fill the centers of the rosettes with red currant jelly, using a salt spoon or the tip of a teaspoon.

Petits Monts Blancs

For meringue suisse
2 egg whites
$\frac{1}{2}$ cup sugar

For chestnut purée
1 lb chestnuts, peeled
about 1 cup milk and 1 cup
   water, mixed
1 vanilla bean
$\frac{1}{4}$ cup sugar
$\frac{1}{4}$ cup water

For filling
Chantilly cream, made with
   1 cup heavy cream, 3–4
   teaspoons sugar and $\frac{1}{2}$
   teaspoon vanilla (see
   page 76)
1 tablespoon grated semisweet
   chocolate

*Pastry bag and $\frac{3}{8}$ and $\frac{1}{8}$ inch
plain tubes*

If you like, 1 can ($8\frac{3}{4}$ oz) sweetened chestnut purée can be substituted for the fresh chestnut purée. Makes 12–16 Monts Blancs.

Method
Set oven at very low (250°F– 275°F). Brush baking sheets with oil and sprinkle with flour; bang the sheets on the table to distribute the flour evenly. Or, line baking sheets with non-stick silicone paper.

Make meringue suisse as for meringues Chantilly (see page 76) and put into a pastry bag fitted with a $\frac{3}{8}$ inch plain tube. Pipe the mixture onto the prepared baking sheets in spirals to make 3 inch rounds. Bake in the heated oven for 35–45 minutes or until the meringues are dry and crisp. Let cool slightly, then transfer to a wire rack to cool completely.

To make the chestnut purée: put the chestnuts in a pan with a mixture of half milk and half water, and the vanilla bean. Cover and simmer 20–30 minutes or until tender. Remove vanilla bean, drain and reserve the liquid. Sieve the chestnuts to a purée through a food mill or with a potato masher; cool.

Dissolve $\frac{1}{4}$ cup sugar in the $\frac{1}{4}$ cup water, bring to a boil and cool. Beat this syrup into the sieved chestnuts and add 1–2 tablespoons reserved cooking liquid to make a purée that is thick enough to pipe. Put into a pastry bag fitted with an $\frac{1}{8}$ inch plain tube and pipe around the edge of the meringue rounds to form a nest. Fill the center with Chantilly cream and sprinkle the cream with grated chocolate.

French Flan Pastry

Sift the flour with the salt onto a board or marble slab and make a large well in the center. Into this put the butter, softened, sugar, egg yolks and vanilla; work all together with the fingertips of one hand until the mixture is smooth. Gradually draw in the flour and work with the hand to form a smooth dough. Chill 1 hour, then roll out and line the flan ring.

If the pastry dough is too stiff to roll, leave it at room temperature to soften for 5– 10 minutes before rolling.

Bake blind in a moderately hot oven (375°F) for 15–20 minutes or until the pastry shell is lightly browned.

To peel chestnuts: prick the shells with a knife. Put nuts in a pan of cold water and bring to a boil. Take from heat and peel the nuts while still hot, taking off the outer and inner skins.

HOW TO COOK IN A CASSEROLE

The ancient art of cooking in a casserole has been rediscovered by smart cooks who know that casseroles are the easy answer to combining the roles of cook and hostess. They are good-natured dishes which take kindly to being kept waiting and are often better when prepared ahead and reheated because the flavors have time to mellow.

A casserole is served in the dish in which it is cooked. Traditionally this was made of earthenware, suited only to baking in the oven, so the ingredients were not browned first on top of the stove. Today there are many flameproof casseroles so that meat or poultry can be browned first before baking in the oven. If you want to use an earthenware pot for such a recipe, brown meat and vegetables in a separate pan, then transfer them to the pot.

Most casseroles are baked in the oven, but some may be entirely cooked on top of the stove instead — this tends to reduce the liquid too rapidly, so keep an eye on the pot to be sure it does not become too dry and the ingredients do not stick to the bottom.

As a rough guide, a casserole of cut-up ingredients to serve 4 people will take 25–30 minutes to reheat in a moderate (350°F) oven. Large pieces of solid meat should be reheated for a longer time at a lower temperature.

Sauté the halibut steak and eggplant before baking with rice; garnish with lemon wedges dipped in chopped parsley

Halibut Casserole

2 lb fresh halibut steak
    (1–1½ inches thick)
¾ cup rice
¼ cup seasoned flour (made
    with ¼ teaspoon salt and
    pinch of pepper)
about ½ cup olive oil
1 medium eggplant, sliced but
    unpeeled
2 onions, chopped
3 cloves of garlic, crushed
3 tomatoes, peeled, seeded and
    chopped
2 tablespoons capers
½ teaspoon ground cumin
salt and pepper
juice of 1 lemon
½ cup white wine
½ teaspoon paprika

For garnish
¼ cup chopped parsley
1 lemon, cut in wedges

Method

Cook the rice in boiling salted water for 12 minutes or until tender. Drain it and rinse in hot water to remove the starch. Coat the halibut with seasoned flour and sauté in half the olive oil in a large frying pan for 2 minutes on each side or until lightly browned. Take out, add the eggplant slices, a few at a time, and brown on both sides, adding more oil as needed. Arrange the browned eggplant slices in the bottom of a large casserole. Add the onions and garlic to the remaining olive oil in the frying pan and sauté until brown.

Take from the heat, add the tomatoes, capers, rice and cumin with salt and pepper to taste and spread the mixture over the eggplant. Place the halibut on top, sprinkle with lemon juice, salt and pepper and add the white wine. Sprinkle the fish with paprika, cover and bake in a moderate-ly hot oven (375°F) for 25–35 minutes, depending on the thickness of the fish (it should flake easily when tested with a fork).

Garnish with lemon wedges dipped in chopped parsley before serving.

Fish Casserole Florentine

1½ lb flounder or other white
    fish fillets
1 lb fresh spinach or 2 packages
    frozen spinach, thawed
2 tablespoons butter
thick béchamel sauce, made
    with 3 tablespoons butter,
    3 tablespoons flour and
    1½ cups milk (infused with
    slice of onion, bay leaf,
    6 peppercorns and blade
    of mace)
¼ cup grated Gruyère or
    Cheddar cheese
¼ cup browned breadcrumbs

Method

Wash the fresh spinach thoroughly and cook it in boiling salted water for 5 minutes or until tender, or cook the frozen spinach according to the package directions. Drain the spinach, press with a plate to extract all the water.

Heat the butter in the pan and sauté the spinach for 1–2 minutes until all moisture has evaporated. Spread the spinach in a shallow buttered casserole. Fold the ends of the fish fillets under to form a rectangle and lay on spinach.

Spoon the béchamel sauce over the fish and spinach to coat them completely. Sprinkle with cheese and breadcrumbs and bake in a moderate oven (350°F) for 15–20 minutes or until browned. The liquid produced by the fish during cooking is absorbed by the thick sauce.

Cioppino

2 medium Dungeness crabs,
    cleaned
2 quarts clams
2 quarts mussels
¾ lb large shrimps
1 onion, sliced
¼ cup oil
3 tomatoes, peeled, seeded
    and finely chopped or 1 cup
    canned tomato purée
1 cup white wine
2 cloves of garlic, crushed
3 tablespoons chopped parsley
salt
black pepper, freshly ground
3 cups water

There are many versions of this famous San Francisco dish. If fresh or frozen crabs in the shell are not available, substitute 1 cup crab meat and add it to the stew 5 minutes before serving.

Method

Chop the legs and claws from the crabs with a cleaver or large knife and chop the bodies in four. Scrub the clams and mussels thoroughly, discarding any that are open and do not close when tapped.

In a flameproof casserole fry the onion in the oil until soft. Add the tomatoes or tomato purée, wine, garlic, parsley, seasoning and water, cover and simmer 30 minutes.

Lay the pieces of crab in the bottom of another large flameproof casserole, add the mussels and clams and put the shrimps on top. Pour over the tomato mixture, cover and simmer 15–20 minutes or until all the clam and mussel shells open. If using live crab, the shells must turn bright red. If not, cook 5 minutes longer. Taste for seasoning; serve with sourdough bread.

Tomato paste is an essential ingredient of chicken casserole italienne

Chicken Casserole Italienne

3½–4 lb roasting chicken
2 tablespoons butter
1 onion, finely chopped
1½ tablespoons tomato paste
1½ cups stock (made from the giblets)
salt and pepper
bouquet garni
1 cup (¼ lb) mushrooms
1 teaspoon cornstarch, or arrowroot mixed to a paste with 1 tablespoon stock or water
½ cup cooked ham, cut in julienne strips
2 tablespoons chopped parsley

Method
In a large flameproof casserole or Dutch oven brown chicken slowly on all sides in butter.

Add onion to casserole and cook slowly until golden brown. Stir in tomato paste and stock, season, add bouquet garni and bring to a boil. Cover casserole tightly and continue cooking on top of the stove or in a moderate oven (350°F) for about 1 hour or until the bird is tender. Add mushrooms 15 minutes before the end of cooking.

Take out the chicken and keep hot. Remove bouquet garni. Thicken the sauce by stirring in the cornstarch or arrowroot paste. Take the pot from heat as soon as it comes to a boil if using arrowroot, or simmer 2 minutes if using cornstarch. Add the ham and taste sauce for seasoning. Carve the chicken into neat pieces and replace in the casserole. Reheat if necessary, sprinkle with parsley and serve.

Chicken Béarnaise

3½–4 lb roasting chicken, cut in pieces
3–4 tablespoons butter, or bacon drippings
1 large onion, sliced
¼ lb piece of bacon, diced
6–8 small carrots, quartered
½ cup white wine or stock
salt and pepper
3 tomatoes, peeled, seeded and sliced
2 cloves of garlic, crushed
2 tablespoons heavy cream (optional)
2 tablespoons chopped parsley (for garnish)

Method
Blanch the onion, bacon and carrots separately by putting them in a pan of cold water, bringing to a boil and draining.

In a flameproof casserole heat the butter or bacon drippings and sauté chicken pieces slowly until golden brown on all sides. Spread the carrots in bottom of casserole, put chicken on top with the onion and bacon. Pour over the wine or stock and season to taste. Cover and bake in a moderate oven (350°F) for ½ hour or until the chicken is almost tender.

Add tomatoes and garlic to the casserole. Cook 15 minutes more or until chicken and carrots are tender. Just before serving, taste the sauce for seasoning; pour cream (if used) over the chicken and sprinkle with chopped parsley.

The French province of **Béarn** in the Pyrenees is well known for its good food and wines. But its most famous namesake, sauce Béarnaise, is believed not to have originated in Béarn at all, but to be the creation of the chef of the restaurant Pavillon Henri IV at St. Germain near Paris. One of the nicknames for Henri IV was the 'grand Béarnais' and the sauce was named after him.

Béarn is also known for its substantial vegetable soups and for the historic Poule au Pot d'Henri IV, another dish named after the king who declared in 1598: 'If God grant me the usual length of life, I hope to make France so prosperous that every peasant will have a chicken in his pot on Sunday'.

To Brown a Chicken
After heating butter in a large, flameproof casserole or Dutch oven, allow at least 10 minutes for browning as a chicken has little or no fat between the skin and flesh and, if browned quickly, it tends to become dry. Always start by browning the breast, first on one side, then on the other and finish with the back. This way there is no danger of the breast becoming discolored if the butter starts to scorch, and the chicken will be the right way up for cooking.

Casserole of Rock Cornish Game Hens

4 rock Cornish game hens
2 tablespoons butter, or oil
1 carrot, diced
1 turnip, diced
2 onions, diced
2–3 stalks of celery, diced
1½ cups stock
bouquet garni
½ cup red wine
salt and pepper
glazed onions (to garnish)

Method
In a flameproof casserole melt butter and slowly brown the hens on all sides. Take them out and keep hot.

Add vegetables to the pot and cook them slowly until all the fat is absorbed and they are lightly browned. Add the stock, bring to a boil and put in the hens with bouquet garni and red wine, that has been flamed.

To flame the wine: heat it gently in a small pan and, as soon as it boils, set a match to it. When the flame burns out, the alcohol will have evaporated.

Add seasoning, cover pot tightly and cook on top of the stove or in a moderately hot oven (375°F) for 35 minutes or until hens are very tender. Baste often with the liquid.

Remove bouquet garni before serving and garnish with glazed onions (see page 98).

Chicken Bonne Femme

3½–4 lb roasting chicken
2 tablespoons butter
12 baby onions, or scallions
¼ lb piece of bacon, cut in short
    strips
1 cup (¼ lb) quartered
    mushrooms
1 tablespoon flour
2–2½ cups stock
bouquet garni
3 medium potatoes, or 8–10
    small new potatoes
salt and pepper
2 tablespoons chopped parsley
    (for garnish)

This dish can be made with pieces of chicken, but the flavor is better if a whole chicken is used.

Method
In a large flameproof casserole heat the butter and, when foaming, put in the chicken, breast down. Brown the bird all over on a low heat for about 15 minutes (see box on page 87).

Blanch the onions and bacon separately by putting in cold water, bringing to a boil and draining.

Take the chicken from the casserole, add onions, bacon and mushrooms and cook until brown, stirring occasionally.

Stir flour into the casserole, pour in the stock and bring to a boil. Replace the chicken, add bouquet garni, cover casserole and bake in a moderate oven (350°F) for about 1 hour.

Peel medium-sized potatoes and cut them in four, trimming the sharp edges; peel new potatoes and leave them whole. Add the potatoes to the casserole 30 minutes before the end of cooking.

When potatoes and chicken are tender, remove chicken and bouquet garni, cut chicken into serving pieces and return to pot. Taste sauce for seasoning and sprinkle with parsley before serving.

Chicken Waterzoi

3½–4 lb roasting chicken
3 carrots, cut in julienne
    strips
1 medium onion, cut in
    julienne strips
2 leeks (white part only), cut
    in julienne strips
2 tablespoons butter
salt and pepper
pinch of sugar
1 cup white wine
4 parsley roots or 1 cup parsley
    stems
1½–2 cups chicken stock
2 teaspoons chopped tarragon
    or parsley

For liaison
2 teaspoons arrowroot
2 egg yolks
½ cup heavy cream

Trussing needle and string

Chicken Waterzoi is a Flemish dish that is a cross between a soup and a stew. It is usually served in bowls with plenty of bread and a spoon for the sauce.

Method
Melt half the butter in a small flameproof casserole, add the carrots, onion and leeks, cover and cook gently for 1 minute. Add the seasoning, sugar and half the wine and bring to a boil. Cover and cook in a moderate oven (350°F) for 10 minutes or until the wine has evaporated.

Scrape the parsley roots or wash the stems and tie with string or a piece of cheesecloth.

Season inside the chicken and truss it.

Spread the remaining butter in a deep flameproof casserole, add the chicken and pour in the stock and remaining wine. Add the parsley roots or stems and the chopped tarragon or parsley.

Scatter the vegetables over the chicken, cover with buttered foil and the lid and bring to a boil. Lower the oven temperature to 325°F and cook the chicken for 1¼–1½ hours or until it is very tender and no pink juice runs out when the thigh is pricked with a fork.

Take out the chicken, carve it and arrange in a bowl or deep serving dish. Lift out the parsley roots or stems, discarding the string or cheesecloth, and work through a sieve or purée in a blender with a little of the cooking liquid. Stir this purée into the remaining liquid in the casserole.

For liaison: mix the arrowroot with the egg yolks and stir in the cream. Add a little hot liquid and stir this liaison into the remaining liquid in the casserole. Heat gently, stirring, until the sauce thickens enough to coat the back of a spoon, but do not boil because it will curdle. Taste the sauce for seasoning and spoon over the chicken. Sprinkle with chopped tarragon or parsley just before serving.

Spanish Chicken Casserole

4–5 lb roasting chicken or
    fowl
1 onion, sliced
2 carrots, sliced
2 stalks of celery, sliced
2 tomatoes, peeled, seeded
    and chopped or 1 cup
    canned tomatoes, crushed
6 cups water
pinch of saffron soaked in
    ½ cup hot water for
    20 minutes
clove of garlic, crushed
salt and pepper
small head of cabbage, cut in
    8 wedges
1 tablespoon chopped parsley
    (for garnish)

Method
Put the chicken or fowl in a flameproof casserole with the vegetables, water, saffron and its liquid, garlic and seasoning. Cover, bring to a boil and simmer 1¼ hours for the roasting chicken or 1½–2 hours for the fowl or until the bird is tender and no pink juice runs out when the thigh is pricked with a fork. Take out the bird and keep warm.

Work the cooking liquid with the vegetables through a sieve or purée them in a blender. Return to the pan with the cabbage and simmer 10 minutes or until the cabbage is tender.

Carve the bird, add to the pan and taste for seasoning. Serve the bird in the casserole or transfer to a bowl and sprinkle with chopped parsley. Serve with boiled rice.

Spanish chicken casserole, sprinkled with chopped parsley, may be served from the casserole or in a deep dish

Game Casserole

2–3 lb venison, moose, or bear,
   without bone
1 teaspoon salt
¼ teaspoon freshly ground
   black pepper
½ teaspoon crushed bay leaf
½ teaspoon rosemary
1½–2 cups milk
½ lb salt pork
2 tablespoons flour
1 teaspoon paprika
1 tablespoon oil
2 tablespoons butter
2 large onions, finely sliced
2½ cups well-flavored stock
1 cup red wine
½ cup sour cream
juice of ½ lemon

This dish must be started at
least 24 hours before cooking.

Method
Cut meat in 1 inch cubes, removing any fat. Place in a
bowl, sprinkle with salt, pepper and herbs and pour over
the milk. Cover and refrigerate
24 hours, turning occasionally.

Blanch the pork by putting
in cold water and bringing to a
boil. Drain and dice it. Drain
milk from meat, and pat dry
with paper towels. Mix the
flour and paprika together and
sprinkle over the meat to
coat each piece.

In a flameproof casserole,
heat oil and fry the salt pork
until brown. Remove it, discard all but 2 tablespoons
fat, add the butter and, when
foaming, brown the meat
quickly all over, a few pieces
at a time. Remove meat from
pot with a slotted spoon,
add onions, lower the heat
and cook slowly, stirring until
golden.

Add the stock and wine and
bring to a boil. Return meat to
the casserole, cover and
simmer very gently on top of
the stove or in a moderately
low oven (325°F) for 2 hours

or until meat is very tender.

Mix sour cream and lemon
juice together and stir into the
casserole, off the heat. Heat
almost to a boil. Taste for
seasoning and serve at once
with mashed potatoes or
chestnut purée (see page 98).
Watchpoint: if the sour cream
is boiled, it will curdle.

Squabs with Raisins

4 squabs
8 slices of bacon, cut in short
   strips
3–4 tablespoons butter
salt and pepper
1½–2 cups brown stock
16 small onions
1 teaspoon sugar (for sprinkling)
½ cup seedless raisins

Method
Split the squabs and cut away
the backbone with poultry
shears. Blanch the bacon by
putting in a pan of cold
water, bringing to a boil and
draining. In a skillet melt the
butter and fry the bacon until
crisp. Take out bacon and
reserve. Add the squabs to the
pan and brown slowly on the
skin side only. Remove and
arrange them in a flame-
proof casserole. Add the
bacon, season with salt and
pepper and barely cover with
stock. Bring to a boil, cover
tightly and bake in a moderately low oven (325°F)
for 1–2½ hours or until very
tender.

Sauté the onions in the
skillet, adding a sprinkling of
sugar to help them brown.
Add to the casserole after
squabs have cooked 30 minutes. Soak the raisins in hot
water until plump, drain and
add to the casserole 15 minutes before serving. At the
end of cooking, the gravy

should be well reduced,
brown and sticky.
Watchpoint: to make good
gravy, jellied stock is essential,
otherwise it will need thickening with kneaded butter or
arrowroot.

Brown Stock

Fry 3 lb beef bones, or mixed
beef and veal bones, gently
in a large kettle for 15–20
minutes, turning occasionally.
After first 10 minutes add 2
onions, 2 carrots, 1 stalk of
celery, all quartered, and
brown them. Add a large
bouquet garni, 6 pepper-
corns, 1 teaspoon salt, and
3–4 quarts water to come
about two-thirds above the
bones. Half cover the pan,
simmer 4–5 hours until the
stock is reduced by about half.
When cool, this will be a
good jellied stock.

The flavor of casseroles is
greatly improved by a good
brown or white bone stock,
or chicken stock. The recipes
in this lesson use brown stock.

Casserole of Duck with Apples

4–5 lb duck
4 dessert apples, pared, cored
   and sliced
1 tablespoon oil
salt and pepper
1 cup cider

Method
In a shallow flameproof casserole heat the oil and brown
the duck on all sides. Be sure
to do this slowly for 20–25
minutes over medium heat so
the fat is extracted from the
duck, preventing the finished
dish from being greasy.

Remove the duck from the
pot and let cool slightly.
Divide the duck into four, first
cutting along the breastbone
with a sharp knife. With
poultry shears, cut down
through the breastbone and
either side of the backbone;
divide each half in two
diagonally between wing and
leg. Trim the pieces neatly.

Pour off all but 2 table-
spoons fat from the pot and
add the sliced apples, arrang-
ing them in a neat layer. Lay
the duck pieces on top,
sprinkle with seasoning and
pour over the cider. Cover and
cook in a moderate oven
(350°F) for 30–40 minutes
or until the duck is tender. If
the apples produce a great
deal of juice, remove the lid
during the last 15 minutes
cooking so the liquid
evaporates.

Two substantial casseroles for a hungry family are, far left: beef and corn; left: lamb and tomato

Beef and Corn Casserole

2–2½ lb chuck steak
2–3 tablespoons oil or beef
   drippings
2 medium onions, sliced
1 tablespoon flour
1½ tablespoons tomato paste
2–2½ cups stock
bouquet garni
salt and pepper
2 ears of yellow corn, or
   1 small can corn kernels
2–3 ripe tomatoes, peeled,
   seeded and sliced
1 tablespoon chopped parsley

Method

Cut meat into 1½ inch cubes and brown quickly in the oil or beef drippings in a flame-proof casserole. Take out the meat, add onions and brown over moderate heat. Stir in the flour and add tomato paste, stock and bouquet garni. Season and stir until boiling.

Replace the meat (there should be just enough gravy to cover the pieces), cover the pot and simmer on top of the stove or in a moderately low oven (325°F) for 1½ hours.

If using fresh corn, cut kernels from corn cobs with a sharp knife. This should make about 1 cup kernels. If using canned corn, drain.

Remove the bouquet garni from the meat, stir in the corn and sliced tomatoes. Cover and continue cooking for 30 minutes or until the steak is very tender. At the end of this time the gravy should be well reduced. Taste for seasoning, sprinkle with parsley and serve.

Lamb and Tomato Casserole

2–3 lb neck of lamb, sliced
salt and pepper
1 teaspoon paprika
2–3 tablespoons butter
2 onions, thinly sliced
1 can (1 lb) tomatoes or
   4 fresh tomatoes, peeled,
   seeded and chopped
1 teaspoon tomato paste
   (optional)
3–4 tablespoons sour cream, or
   yogurt
1 tablespoon chopped parsley

Method

Rub the meat with salt, pepper, and paprika. In a flame-proof casserole heat the butter and brown meat on both sides. Take out, add onions and brown also. Replace the meat and add tomatoes. When using fresh tomatoes, cook them to a pulp in a separate pan before adding to the casserole and add tomato paste if they are not a bright red color.

Cover the pot tightly and cook slowly in a low oven (300°F) for 2–3 hours or until the meat is very tender. Before serving, stir the sour cream or yogurt into the juices in the casserole, taste for seasoning and spoon this sauce over the meat. Sprinkle with parsley and serve with mashed or boiled potatoes, and onion ragoût (see page 98).

Boeuf Braisé Flamande
(Flemish-style Braised Beef)

3–3½ lb round, rump or sirloin
   tip of beef
2 tablespoons oil
2 onions, sliced
2 carrots, sliced
2 stalks of celery, sliced
3 leeks, sliced
1 cup ale
1 cup stock
bouquet garni
1 clove of garlic, crushed
1 teaspoon tomato paste
kneaded butter, made with
   2 tablespoons butter and
   1 tablespoon flour
1 tablespoon chopped parsley

For tomato coulis
4 tomatoes, peeled, sliced
   and seeded
1 tablespoon oil
1 Bermuda or large onion,
   sliced in rounds
salt and pepper

Method
In a deep flameproof casserole heat the oil and brown the meat thoroughly on all sides. Take out, add the vegetables, turn down the heat, cover and cook gently for 5–7 minutes or until the oil is absorbed. Replace the meat, add the ale, stock, bouquet garni, garlic and tomato paste, cover tightly and braise in a moderately low oven (325°F) for 1½–2 hours or until the meat is tender.

Take out the beef and keep warm. Strain the cooking liquid into a pan, bring to a boil and whisk in the kneaded butter, a piece at a time, to thicken the sauce. Taste for seasoning.

To make the tomato coulis: heat the oil and fry the onion until browned. Add the tomatoes, season, cover and cook 2–3 minutes until the tomatoes are just soft. Spoon the coulis down the center of a warm platter.

Carve the beef in $\frac{3}{8}$ inch slices and arrange them, overlapping, on the tomato coulis. Spoon over a little of the sauce and serve the rest separately. Sprinkle the dish with parsley and serve with mashed potatoes.

Coulis is French for a purée of tomatoes, or any liquid pulp, used to flavor ragoûts and stews. The term may also be given to the strained juice of meat, fish or poultry, thickened with bread, flour or cornstarch.

Casserole of Liver

4–6 slices of lamb, or beef, liver
3–4 tablespoons butter
8 slices of bacon, diced
1 cup (¼ lb) mushrooms
3 medium onions, sliced
1 tablespoon flour
2 cups beef stock
salt and pepper
12 ripe olives, pitted
squeeze of lemon juice

Method
In a skillet heat 1 tablespoon butter and sauté the bacon until crisp. Take out and reserve; add the liver and sauté 2 minutes on each side until brown. Take out and arrange the slices in a casserole.

Wipe out the skillet, melt remaining butter and sauté the mushrooms for 2 minutes or until soft; take out and set aside. Sauté the onions until golden brown and add with the bacon to the liver in casserole.

Sprinkle flour into the skillet and stir to make a roux. Pour on the stock and bring to a boil, stirring. Season, strain into the casserole, cover and cook gently on top of the stove (if using a flameproof casserole) or in a moderate oven (350°F) for 40–50 minutes or until liver is very tender. Add mushrooms and olives, sprinkle over the lemon juice and cook 10 minutes more. Taste the sauce for seasoning and serve.

Steak Mexicaine

2–2½ lb round or chuck steak
2 tablespoons flour
3 tablespoons oil
3 onions, finely sliced
2 cloves of garlic, crushed
1 cup tomato sauce (see right)
1 cup beef stock
1½ tablespoons chili powder
salt and pepper

Method

Coat steak with flour. In a shallow flameproof casserole, heat the oil and brown steak on both sides. Take it out, add onions and garlic and brown. Stir in tomato sauce, stock, chili powder, salt and pepper and put back the steak, immersing it in the liquid. Cover pot tightly and bake in a moderately low oven (325°F) for 1½–2 hours or until the steak is very tender. Taste for seasoning.

Tomato Sauce

1 can (1 lb) tomatoes or 4 fresh tomatoes
2 tablespoons butter
1½ tablespoons flour
1½ cups stock, or water
bouquet garni
salt and pepper
pinch of sugar
1 teaspoon tomato paste (optional)

Method

In a saucepan melt the butter, stir in the flour and blend in stock or water, off the heat. Bring to a boil, stirring.

Wipe fresh tomatoes (peel only if you will be puréeing in blender), and whether fresh or canned, cut in half and squeeze to remove seeds. Strain seeds to remove juice. Add tomatoes and juice to sauce with bouquet garni. Season, add sugar and tomato paste to strengthen flavor, if you like. Cover pan and simmer gently for 30 minutes or until tomatoes are pulpy.

Remove bouquet garni; work sauce through a strainer (or purée in a blender). Return to rinsed pan and adjust seasoning; simmer 5 minutes or until it is the right consistency.
Note: a tomato sauce should be of flowing, rather than coating consistency. For a good gloss, stir in 1 tablespoon butter before serving.

Pork and Beef Casserole

1½ lb pork boneless shoulder
¾ lb beef chuck or round steak
2 tablespoons oil
1 onion, chopped
2 cloves of garlic, crushed
½ lb chorizo or pepperoni sausage, sliced
1 fresh or canned jalapeño or serrano chili
salt and pepper
3–4 cups water
1½ lb sweet potatoes, cut in chunks
2 green peppers, cored, seeded and cut in squares
2 red bell peppers, cored, seeded and cut in squares
1 lb yellow squash, thickly sliced

Method

Prepare the chilies (see box). Cut the pork and beef into 1½ inch cubes.

In a flameproof casserole heat the oil and brown the meat on all sides, a few pieces at a time. Take out, add the onion and brown also. Replace the meat, add the garlic, sausage, chilies and seasoning and enough water almost to cover the meat. Cover and simmer 1 hour.

Add the sweet potatoes with more water almost to cover them, cover the pan and simmer 15 minutes longer. Add the peppers and squash and cook 15 minutes longer or until the meat and vegetables are tender.

> **Jalapeño** and **serrano chilies** are both green and pointed in shape. Jalapeño chilies are hotter than serrano; both are available fresh and in cans.
>
> **To prepare fresh chilies:** soak them in cold water for 1 hour to remove some of the hot taste.
> **To prepare canned chilies:** rinse them in cold water and drain, reserving the liquid if necessary.

Ham with Orange

1½–2 inch thick of regular ham steak
2 oranges
¼ cup brown sugar
½ teaspoon ground cinnamon
¼ teaspoon ground cloves
½ teaspoon ground allspice
¼ teaspoon ground black pepper
½ cup fresh orange juice

Method

Lay the ham in a shallow, flameproof casserole. Cut the unpeeled oranges in thick slices and arrange on top of ham.

Combine the sugar with the spices and black pepper and spread on top of the ham. Pour over the orange juice, cover and bake in a moderate oven (350°F) for 45 minutes or until the ham is tender, basting from time to time during cooking. Remove the lid for the last 15 minutes so the sugar and orange juice form a glaze.

Veal casserole bolognese is a rich dish cooked in red wine

Casseroled Pork Chops

4 thick, or 8 medium, pork
   chops
2 tablespoons oil
1 small onion, finely chopped
1 tablespoon flour
1½ cups stock
bouquet garni
2 teaspoons tomato paste
1 clove of garlic, crushed
salt and pepper
¼ lb piece of bacon, cut in
   short strips
12 small onions

Method

In a flameproof casserole heat
oil and brown the chops on
both sides. Add the chopped
onion and sprinkle over the
flour. Turn chops to coat them
in the mixture and fry 1 minute. Take from heat and barely
cover with stock. Add bouquet garni, tomato paste and
garlic. Season lightly, cover
pot tightly and bake in a
moderate oven (350°F) for 30
minutes.

Blanch the bacon and small
onions separately by putting
them in a pan of cold water,
bringing to a boil and draining.
Add to the pork chops, push-
ing onions down so they are
immersed in liquid, and continue cooking 30 minutes or
until onions, bacon and chops
are tender. Remove bouquet
garni, taste for seasoning,
and serve.

Veal Chops with Mustard

4 veal chops
¼–½ lb piece of bacon, diced
2 tablespoons bacon drippings,
   or oil
4 medium onions, quartered
1 tablespoon flour
2½ cups stock
bouquet garni
salt
black pepper, freshly ground
¼ cup heavy cream
2 tablespoons Dijon-style
   mustard
1 tablespoon chopped parsley

Method

Blanch the bacon by putting it
in a pan of cold water, bringing to a boil and draining.

Heat the bacon drippings or
oil in a flameproof casserole
and brown the chops on both
sides. Take them out, add the
bacon and onions and fry until
brown. Take from the heat,
stir in flour and pour in stock.
Bring to a boil, stirring, replace the chops and add bouquet garni and season to
taste. Cover casserole and
bake in a moderate oven
(350°F) for 1 hour or until
the chops are very tender.

Remove the bouquet garni.
Mix the cream with the mustard and parsley and stir into
the casserole, off the heat.
Taste for seasoning and reheat
before serving.

Veal Casserole Bolognese

1½–2 lb leg or shoulder of veal
2 tablespoons oil
1 onion, chopped
1 tablespoon flour
1 cup red wine
1½ cups stock
2 cloves of garlic, crushed
1 tablespoon grated orange
   rind
2 tomatoes, peeled, seeded
   and chopped or 1 cup canned
   Italian-style tomatoes,
   crushed
bouquet garni
salt and pepper

Method

Cut the veal into 1½ inch
cubes, discarding the fat.

In a flameproof casserole
heat the oil and brown the
veal on all sides over medium
heat, a few pieces at a time.
Remove, add the onion and
brown it also. Stir in the flour,
cook ½ minute and add the
wine, stock, garlic, orange
rind, tomatoes, bouquet
garni and seasoning. Replace
the meat, bring the casserole
to a boil, cover and cook in a
moderate oven (350°F) for
1½–2 hours or until the veal is
very tender.

Taste for seasoning and
serve.

Lima Bean Casserole

2 lb lima beans, shelled, or
   1 package frozen baby limas
1 cup (¼ lb) sliced mushrooms
2 tablespoons butter
¾ cup sour cream
2 teaspoons marjoram
salt and pepper (to taste)

Method

Cook fresh beans in boiling
salted water for 15–20 minutes or until just tender and
drain. Cook frozen beans
according to the package
directions, and drain.

Sauté the mushrooms in
the butter until soft. Combine
the beans, mushrooms, sour
cream and marjoram in a casserole with salt and pepper to
taste, cover and bake in a
moderate oven (350°F) for
20 minutes. Serve the beans
in the casserole.

Zucchini and Corn Casserole

1½ lb zucchini, sliced
1 cup cooked corn kernels
¼ cup butter
8–9 scallions, finely sliced
1 clove of garlic, crushed
1 cup heavy cream
4 eggs, beaten to mix
1 cup grated Cheddar cheese
salt and pepper

Method

Melt butter in a skillet, add
scallions and fry until soft.
Add the zucchini, cover and
cook over low heat until zucchini are almost tender but not
brown, stirring occasionally.
Mix them with well-drained
corn, pour into a buttered
baking dish and sprinkle over
the garlic.

Stir the cream into the
eggs, add half the cheese and
season to taste. Pour this
mixture into the baking dish,
sprinkle top with remaining
cheese and bake in a mod-
erate oven (350°F) for 30–
35 minutes or until the egg
mixture is just set.

Eggplant Casserole

2 medium eggplants, sliced
salt
about 6 tablespoons oil
1 onion, chopped
2 tomatoes, peeled, seeded
   and chopped or $1\frac{1}{2}$ cups
   canned Italian-style
   tomatoes, crushed
2 cloves of garlic, crushed
1 teaspoon basil
black pepper, freshly ground
$1\frac{1}{2}$ cups (about $\frac{1}{2}$ lb) cooked
   ham, diced
$\frac{1}{2}$ lb mozzarella cheese, thinly
   sliced
$\frac{1}{4}$ cup grated Parmesan cheese

Method

Sprinkle the eggplant slices with salt and let stand 30 minutes to draw out the juices (dégorger). Rinse them and dry on paper towels.

Brush the eggplant slices with oil, set them on an oiled baking sheet and bake in a moderate oven (350°F) for 15 minutes or until lightly browned. Turn them over, brush again with oil and brown the other sides.

In a skillet fry the onion in 2 tablespoons oil until soft. Add the tomatoes, garlic, basil and seasoning and simmer until thick, stirring occasionally; add the ham.

In a casserole layer the eggplant slices with the mozzarella cheese and tomato mixture, ending with a layer of eggplant. Sprinkle the top with grated Parmesan cheese and bake in a moderate oven (350°F) for 25–30 minutes or until browned.

Lima Beans Marie-Anne

2 cups shelled baby lima beans
½ lb baby carrots
1 tablespoon butter

For poulette sauce
2 tablespoons butter
2 tablespoons flour
1½ cups well-flavored chicken stock
salt and pepper
1 egg yolk
2–3 tablespoons heavy cream
½ teaspoon savory
1 tablespoon chopped parsley

Serve with lamb and veal.

Method

Cook the beans in boiling salted water for 15 20 minutes or until just tender, drain, refresh and drain again. If the carrots are large, quarter them; cook in boiling salted water for 15 minutes or until just tender and drain them. In a saucepan or flameproof casserole melt butter, add beans and carrots, cover and keep warm.

To make the poulette sauce: melt the butter, stir in the flour and cook over medium heat until the roux is pale straw-colored. Take from heat, pour in stock, then bring to a boil, stirring. Season to taste and simmer 2–3 minutes or until sauce is the consistency of heavy cream. Mix the egg yolk with the cream, stir in a little of the hot sauce and stir this liaison with the herbs back into the remaining sauce.

Heat the sauce until it thickens slightly but do not let it boil because it will curdle. Pour it over the beans and carrots and heat them, until very hot, shaking the pan so sauce and vegetables mix well. Serve in the casserole or transfer to a hot serving dish.

Lima beans Marie-Anne are ideal with lamb and veal dishes

CASSEROLE ACCOMPANIMENTS

Casseroles have the advantage of combining many ingredients in one pot, so few accompaniments are necessary. However, something is needed to absorb the gravy. Here are some suggestions to escape the boiled potatoes and rice routine.

Brown Rice

1 cup brown rice
¼ cup butter
salt and pepper

Brown rice is simply white rice, whose nutritive outer layers have not been removed by milling. It has an interesting, nutty flavor that blends well with chicken.

Method
Cook rice in plenty of boiling salted water for 20–25 minutes or according to package directions – it should be tender but still have a definite texture. Drain, wash with hot water to remove the starch and spread in a buttered dish. Dot with remaining butter, sprinkle with a little pepper and place in a very low oven (200°F) for 15–30 minutes to dry and heat. Toss occasionally with a fork.

Lentil Purée

1 cup lentils
1 onion, stuck with 1 clove
1 carrot, cut in rounds
bouquet garni
salt and pepper
little stock (optional)
¼ cup butter
1 stalk of celery, very finely chopped

This is an excellent accompaniment to casseroled pork or veal. Dried peas may be used instead of lentils.

Method
Soak the lentils according to package directions. Drain and combine in a saucepan with onion, carrot, bouquet garni, a little salt and plenty of water. Simmer for 1½ hours or until tender.

Remove bouquet garni and take clove out of onion; work mixture through a sieve or purée in a blender. Reheat and thin with a little stock if purée is too thick. Take from the heat and beat in the butter with pepper to taste. Before serving, stir in chopped celery.

Onion Ragoût

24 small onions, peeled
2 tablespoons butter
1 teaspoon sugar
½ cup white wine, cider or stock

Method
Blanch onions by putting them in a pan of cold water and bringing to a boil. Drain and combine in a casserole with the butter, sugar and wine, cider or stock. Cover tightly and bake in a moderate oven (350°F) for 40–45 minutes or until tender. Serve in the casserole.

Glazed Onions

Cover 18 small onions, peeled, with cold water, add salt and bring to a boil. Drain off the water, add 2–3 tablespoons butter and sprinkle 1 tablespoon sugar over the onions.

Cover and cook gently, shaking the pan occasionally until the onions are tender and golden brown with caramelized sugar — about 10 minutes.

Chestnut Purée

2 lb chestnuts, peeled
1 stalk of celery
bouquet garni
2 cups stock
¼ cup butter
¼ teaspoon allspice
salt and pepper

This purée is delicious with game or pork.

Method
In a saucepan cook chestnuts with celery, bouquet garni and stock until boiling; cover and simmer 45 minutes or until the chestnuts are very tender but not mushy. Drain them, discard the celery and bouquet garni and work chestnuts through a sieve or food mill, or purée in a blender with a little cooking liquid.

Return purée to the pan and beat in the butter over heat. Season with allspice and salt and pepper to taste. The purée should be light and not at all sticky. If too thick, beat in a little of the cooking liquid.

To peel chestnuts: prick the shells with a knife. Put nuts in a pan of cold water and bring to a boil. Take from heat and peel the nuts while still hot, taking off the outer and inner skins.

Sweet Potato Casserole

1½ lb sweet potatoes
grated rind and juice of
    1 orange
¼ cup butter
¼ teaspoon ground cinnamon
¼ teaspoon ground mace
¼ teaspoon ground allspice
salt and pepper
2 tablespoons brown sugar

Serve with pork and duck.

Method

Cook the potatoes, unpeeled, in boiling salted water for 20–25 minutes or until tender. Drain them, peel and mash with a potato masher or work through a ricer.

Beat the potatoes with the orange rind and juice, half the butter, the spices and seasoning until smooth. Spread in a shallow casserole, dot with the remaining butter and sprinkle with sugar. Bake in a hot oven (400°F) until browned.

Polenta Cakes

1 cup coarsely ground yellow
    corn meal
1 quart water
1 teaspoon salt
1 teaspoon paprika
¼ teaspoon cayenne
black pepper, freshly ground
2 tablespoons grated Parmesan
    cheese (optional)
¼ cup butter, or olive oil

Serve with beef and chicken casseroles or with any casserole containing tomato.

Method

Bring water to a boil with salt and gradually stir in the corn meal. Cook the mixture over low heat, stirring often, for 15 minutes or until it comes

away from sides of pan. Beat in paprika and cayenne with black pepper to taste and grated Parmesan cheese, if used. Spread mixture in a greased pan to form a layer ½ inch thick and chill until set. Cut into 2 inch squares or circles and sauté in butter or olive oil until brown on both sides.

Bulgur
or Kasha

1 cup medium, or coarse,
    cracked wheat (bulgur), or
    buckwheat
1 small egg, beaten to mix
2 cups stock, or water
salt and pepper

When this dish is made with buckwheat instead of regular wheat, it becomes the famous kasha. Both bulgur and kasha have a light yet chewy texture that is excellent with beef casseroles.

Method

In a flameproof casserole, combine the wheat with egg and cook over medium heat, stirring constantly, until each grain is dry and separate — this will take 10–15 minutes. Add the stock or water with salt and pepper to taste, cover pot and bake in a moderate oven (350°F) for 20–30 minutes, or until all the liquid is absorbed and the wheat is tender. Leave 15–20 minutes in a warm place or in a very low oven before serving. (This allows the starch grains to contract so the dish is not mushy.)

Herb Dumplings

½ cup self-rising flour
½ cup fresh white breadcrumbs
¼ cup ground beef suet
2 tablespoons chopped mixed
    herbs (chives, thyme,
    parsley, marjoram)
salt and pepper
1 egg, beaten to mix

These dumplings are good with beef or game.

Method

In a bowl combine flour, breadcrumbs, suet, herbs, and salt and pepper to taste. Add enough egg to bind the mixture and shape into balls the size of walnuts. Add 40 minutes before end of cooking time to any casserole dish that has plenty of gravy. Turn dumplings after 20 minutes, so they cook on both sides.

Baked Barley

1 cup pearl barley
1 large onion, chopped
1 cup (¼ lb) sliced mushrooms
    (optional)
5–6 tablespoons butter
2 cups stock
salt and pepper

Method

In a skillet sauté onions, and mushrooms, if used, in butter until they are tender. Stir in the barley and continue cooking until it is browned lightly. Pour the mixture into a buttered casserole and add 1 cup stock.

Cover the casserole and bake in a moderate oven (350°F) for about 30 minutes. Uncover and stir in remaining cup of stock; add salt and pepper to taste. Cover and continue baking until all the liquid is absorbed and the barley is tender.

Lemon Stuffing Balls

¼ cup butter
1 small onion, finely chopped
1 cup fresh white breadcrumbs
2 tablespoons chopped parsley
1 tablespoon grated lemon rind
salt and pepper
1 egg, beaten to mix
¼ cup seasoned flour (made
    with ¼ teaspoon salt and
    pinch of pepper)
¼ cup browned breadcrumbs
deep fat (for frying)

Serve with chicken and veal casseroles.

Method

In a skillet melt butter and fry the onion until soft. Mix onion and butter with the breadcrumbs, parsley and lemon rind in a bowl and add salt and pepper to taste. Stir in enough beaten egg to bind the mixture; roll into balls the size of a walnut. Roll these in seasoned flour, coat with egg and browned breadcrumbs. Fry them a few at a time in hot deep fat (360°F on a fat thermometer) until golden brown. Drain on paper towels.

Salad Clementine is a piquant appetizer (recipe is on page 102)

A Tempting Supper

Take it easy and prepare for dinner well ahead of time. For an appetizer there is a choice of tomato, egg, and anchovy salad or a simple soup. The veal chops with mushrooms and onions can be reheated easily and dessert is a rich Austrian cake made with ground hazelnuts and filled with an apple mixture. Or for a complete contrast, serve orange mousse topped with a lattice of whipped cream.

Veal is one meat that goes well with a white wine. Try a Pouilly Fuissé from southern Burgundy; it's known for its sprightly quality, reasonable cost and adaptability to many dishes. As an American alternative, you might like a good Chardonnay from California that combines the grace and strength needed in a white wine to accompany a meat entrée.

Salad Clementine
or
Soup Georgette

Veal Chops Bonne Femme
Zucchini au Gratin
or
Braised Belgian Endive

Nusskuchen
or
Orange Mousse
∽

White wine – Pouilly Fuissé (Mâconnais)
or Chardonnay (California)

TIMETABLE

Day before
Make and bake the cake for nusskuchen; store in an airtight container. Make the apple filling for the nusskuchen and keep covered.
Hard cook the eggs for salad Clementine but do not refrigerate.

Morning
Peel and sauté the tomatoes for salad Clementine; keep covered. Chop herbs and keep in plastic wrap; make the dressing.
Make the soup but do not add the cream.
Cook the bacon for the veal chops, and cut into lardons; blanch onions for the chops.
Cook the chops, add the potatoes and cook only 10 minutes; leave ready for reheating.
Cook the zucchini, cool, add the egg and cream mixture, cover and keep in the refrigerator ready for baking.
Make the orange mousse, cover tightly and chill.

Assemble equipment for final cooking from 7:15 for dinner around 8 p.m.

Order of Work

7:15
Set oven at hot (400°F).
Split and fill the cake; finish top with confectioner's sugar or melted chocolate. *Or decorate the orange mousse.*

7:30
Bake zucchini until browned and the custard is just set; keep warm.
Soak the anchovies in milk, slice the hard-cooked eggs, complete salad Clementine and chill.

7:45
Reheat the chops on top of the stove, transfer to the serving dish and keep warm.
Reheat the soup and add the light cream.

8:00
Serve the salad Clementine *or the soup Georgette.*

You will find that **cooking times** given in the individual recipes for these dishes have sometimes been adapted in the timetable to help you when cooking and serving this menu as a party meal.

Appetizer

Salad Clementine

6 tomatoes, peeled, halved and seeded
salt and pepper
2 tablespoons oil
6 hard-cooked eggs, sliced
1 tablespoon capers
1 tablespoon sliced gherkin pickles
6 anchovy fillets
2 tablespoons milk

For dressing
2 tablespoons wine vinegar
1 teaspoon dry mustard
6 tablespoons oil
2 tablespoons ketchup
1 tablespoon chopped mixed herbs (parsley, chives and mint)
black pepper, freshly ground

Method
Season the tomatoes lightly with salt and pepper. Sauté them quickly on each side in the oil, remove carefully from the pan and cool.

Arrange the sliced eggs in the bottom of an entrée dish and sprinkle them with capers and gherkin pickles. Place the tomatoes, cut side down, on top.

Split anchovies in half lengthwise and soak them for 15 minutes in the milk to remove excess salt.

Beat together the ingredients for the dressing and add salt and pepper to taste. Drain anchovies and arrange in a lattice pattern over the tomatoes. Spoon over the dressing and chill the salad in the refrigerator for about 1 hour before serving.
Watchpoint: the tomatoes for this dish must be sautéed in oil, even when they are very ripe. If not, they will give off too much juice on standing, after the dressing has been added.

To peel a tomato easily, spear it on a fork and hold over a gas flame or burner so the skin chars

To Peel and Seed Tomatoes

Pour boiling water over the tomatoes, let stand 10 seconds and then drain. This cooks the tomatoes slightly so the skins can be peeled off easily. For 1–2 tomatoes, it may be easier to spear them throuth the core with a fork and hold them over a gas flame or burner for 15–20 seconds, turning until the skin chars slightly all over and the skin peels easily.

To remove tomato seeds before chopping: cut the tomato in half across the sections. Hold the tomato half in the palm of the hand and squeeze firmly so the seeds are forced out. Cut in quarters, strips, or chop the tomatoes according to the recipe.

Alternative Appetizer

Soup Georgette

5–6 ripe tomatoes, peeled
1 small bunch of celery, thinly
 sliced
2 leeks, thinly sliced
3–4 lb carrots, thinly sliced
2 tablespoons butter
2 tablespoons flour
$2\frac{1}{2}$ cups water
pinch of sugar
$\frac{1}{2}$ bay leaf
pinch of nutmeg
salt and pepper
1 teaspoon arrowroot (mixed to
 a paste with 1 tablespoon
 water) – optional
5 tablespoons light cream
1 tablespoon chopped parsley
 (for sprinkling)

Method
Quarter tomatoes, remove seeds and strain them, reserving juice. Cook the celery, leeks and carrots in the butter for a few minutes until soft but not brown. Stir in the flour and add the tomato flesh and juice, water, sugar, bay leaf, nutmeg and seasoning. Stir the mixture until it comes to a boil and simmer for 30 minutes. Work through a sieve, or remove the bay leaf and purée mixture in a blender. Return to the pan to reheat. If the soup needs thickening, stir in the arrowroot paste and bring to a boil. Adjust seasoning, simmer for a few seconds, then stir in the light cream.

Before serving, sprinkle the soup with chopped parsley.

Soup Georgette makes a good alternative appetizer to salad Clementine

For salad Clementine, top peeled halved tomatoes with anchovy fillets

Entrée

Veal Chops Bonne Femme

4 large veal chops
$\frac{1}{2}$ lb piece of bacon
16 small onions, peeled
1 cup ($\frac{1}{4}$ lb) mushrooms
3 tablespoons butter
$1\frac{1}{2}$ tablespoons flour
1 cup stock (use $1\frac{1}{2}$ cups if not using wine)
$\frac{1}{2}$ cup white wine (optional)
salt and pepper
bouquet garni
3 medium potatoes, or 8–10 small new potatoes, peeled
1 tablespoon chopped parsley

Method
Put the bacon in a pan, cover with water and simmer 45 minutes. Let cool in the liquid, then drain. Cut the bacon into lardons (strips $\frac{1}{4}$ inch thick and $1\frac{1}{2}$ inches long). Blanch the onions and drain. Wipe mushrooms with a damp cloth and cut in half or into quarters, depending on the size.

In a skillet heat butter and brown veal chops on both sides. Transfer the chops to a plate, and add mushrooms, onions and bacon to the pan. Sauté until the onions are golden brown, stir in the flour until smooth, add stock and wine and bring to a boil, stirring. Season to taste with salt and pepper, return chops to the skillet and add the bouquet garni. Cover and simmer on top of the stove or in a moderate oven (350°F) for 20 minutes.

Quarter the medium potatoes lengthwise and trim off the sharp corners; leave the small new ones whole. Blanch them and add to the chops. Continue cooking 20 minutes longer or until both potatoes and chops are tender. Remove bouquet garni, taste for seasoning and sprinkle the chops and potatoes with parsley. Serve with zucchini au gratin or braised Belgian endive.

Cut bacon into lardons before browning the veal chops on both sides in butter

Sauté mushrooms, onions and lardons of bacon until golden brown, and stir in flour

Accompaniments to Entrée

Zucchini au Gratin

$1\frac{1}{2}$ lb zucchini
salt
$\frac{1}{2}$ cup water
2 eggs
1 cup heavy cream
$\frac{1}{4}$ cup grated Gruyère cheese
black pepper, freshly ground
1 tablespoon butter

Method
Wipe zucchini with a damp cloth and trim the ends. Cut into $\frac{1}{2}$ inch diagonal slices and put in a pan with water and $\frac{1}{2}$ teaspoon salt. Cover and cook over moderate heat until the water has evaporated and zucchini are almost tender.

Mix the eggs, cream and grated cheese together, reserving 1 tablespoon cheese, and season the mixture with salt and pepper. Transfer zucchini to an ovenproof gratin dish, pour over the cream mixture and sprinkle the top with reserved cheese. Dot the top with small pieces of butter and bake in a hot oven (400°F) for about 10 minutes, or until the egg mixture is just set and the top is golden brown.

Braised Belgian Endive

8 heads of Belgian endive
2 tablespoons butter
salt and pepper
juice of $\frac{1}{2}$ lemon
2 tablespoons water
1 tablespoon finely chopped parsley (for garnish)

Method
Rub the butter over the bottom of a shallow flameproof casserole or skillet. Trim off the bottoms and any damaged outer leaves of the endive and cut the heads into diagonal slices about 1 inch thick. Put them in the pan with salt and pepper to taste, lemon juice and water.

Press a piece of buttered foil on top of the endive and cover with a lid. Cook over low heat for 7–8 minutes or until the endive is tender, shaking the pan occasionally. Sprinkle with chopped parsley and serve.

Serve veal chops bonne femme with zucchini au gratin for an easy supper

Dessert

Nusskuchen

½ cup butter
½ cup sugar
2 eggs
⅓ cup shelled hazelnuts, or
    whole blanched almonds,
    browned and ground
1 teaspoon dry instant coffee
1 tablespoon warm milk
1 cup self-rising flour
pinch of salt

For filling
3 dessert apples
2 tablespoons apricot jam
grated rind and juice of ½ lemon

To decorate
confectioners' sugar (for
    sprinkling), or 2 squares
    (2 oz) semisweet chocolate

8 inch springform pan

Method
Grease and flour the springform pan. Set oven at moderately hot (375°F).

In a bowl cream the butter
and gradually beat in the
sugar until light and fluffy.
Separate the eggs and beat
the yolks into butter and
sugar mixture. Stir in the nuts.
Dissolve the coffee in the
warm milk and set aside;
sift flour and salt together;
beat egg whites until they
hold a stiff peak. Fold the
flour into the creamed mixture in three portions alternately with the coffee-flavor-
ed milk. Fold in the egg whites
and pour the batter into the
prepared pan. Bake in the
heated oven for about 25
minutes or until the cake is
firm to the touch and shrinks
slightly from the sides of the
pan. Remove cake from pan
and cool on a wire rack.

To make the filling: pare,
core and slice the apples and
cook them, covered, in a pan
with the apricot jam, lemon
rind and juice until soft. Let
stand until cool.

Split the cake in half and
sandwich the layers with
the cool apple mixture. Sprinkle the top with confectioners'
sugar, or melt the chocolate
on a heatproof plate over a
pan of hot water and spread
on the cake with a metal
spatula.

*Fill the cake with the cooled
apple mixture*

*Spread the top of the cake
with melted chocolate*

Alternative Filling for Nusskuchen

Melt 3 squares (3 oz) semisweet chocolate on a heatproof plate over a pan of hot
water and let stand until cool
but still liquid.

Stiffly whip 1 cup heavy
cream and fold in the cooled
chocolate. Sandwich the cake
with half the chocolate cream.

Put the remaining choco-
late cream into a pastry bag
fitted with a medium star tube
and decorate the top of the
cake with rosettes of cream.

Alternative Dessert

Orange Mousse

grated rind and juice of
    2 oranges
3 eggs
2 egg yolks
⅓ cup sugar
1 envelope gelatin
juice of 1 lemon
½ cup heavy cream, whipped
    until it holds a soft shape

For decoration
¾ cup heavy cream, stiffly
    whipped
¼ cup slivered almonds,
    browned and chopped

*Glass bowl or soufflé dish
(1½ quart capacity); pastry
bag and medium star tube*

Method
Put the eggs, egg yolks and
sugar into a bowl and beat
until mixed. Set the bowl
over a pan of hot but not
boiling water and beat until
the mixture is thick and light
and leaves a ribbon trail on
itself when the beater is lifted.
If using an electric beater,
no heat is necessary.

Sprinkle the gelatin over
the lemon juice and let stand
5 minutes until spongy. Dissolve the gelatin over a pan of
hot water, and stir into the
egg mixture with the orange
juice and grated rind.

Chill the bowl over a pan of
ice water, stirring gently until
the mixture is on the point of
setting. Fold in the lightly
whipped cream and pour at
once into the bowl or dish.
Cover and chill at least 2 hours
or until set.

A short time before serving,
put the stiffly whipped cream
into the pastry bag fitted with
the star tube and decorate the
mousse with a lattice of
whipped cream; sprinkle the
edge with browned almonds.

> **To brown and grind
> almonds and hazelnuts:**
> blanch and remove skins
> of almonds, if necessary,
> before browning. Bake
> hazelnuts or almonds in a
> moderately hot oven
> (375°F) for 8–10 min-
> utes or until browned.
> To remove skins of hazel-
> nuts, rub them in a rough
> cloth after browning.
> Grind almonds or hazel-
> nuts in a rotary cheese
> grater or a blender.

Apples flavored with apricot and lemon make a refreshing filling for the nusskuchen

COOKING WITH VEGETABLES

Tomatoes, peppers, corn and the many kinds of squash are symbols of summer, although they are available all year. Here are just a few ways to cook these and many other vegetables. Remember, too, that there are more vegetable recipes in the lesson on cooking in a casserole (pages 83–99).

Potage cultivateur is a simple soup made from vegetables in season; serve with croûtons

Potage Cultivateur

$\frac{1}{4}$ lb piece of bacon, diced
2 tablespoons butter
2 carrots, sliced
1 onion, diced
1 small turnip, diced
3 tomatoes, peeled, seeded
    and chopped
2 leeks, thinly sliced
1 cup fresh peas
1 cup fresh lima beans
1 cup green beans, cut in
    $\frac{1}{2}$ inch lengths
1 quart water
salt and pepper

Depending on the season, turnips, peas, leeks and beans can be omitted from the soup.

Method
Blanch the bacon in boiling water for 5 minutes and drain.

In a large kettle melt the butter and fry the carrots, onion and turnip until soft but not browned. Add the tomatoes, leeks, peas, lima beans, green beans, bacon, water and seasoning and bring to a boil. Skim, cover the kettle and simmer 30 minutes, skimming occasionally. Taste for seasoning and serve with croûtons.

Croûtons
Cut several slices of bread into cubes, removing the crusts. Fry the cubes in 3–4 tablespoons hot shallow fat or in deep fat until golden brown; drain on paper towels. Sprinkle lightly with salt.

Potage Bonne Femme

6–8 medium leeks
3 medium potatoes, peeled and
    sliced
5 tablespoons butter
salt and pepper
2 cups milk
2 cups water
2 egg yolks
$\frac{3}{4}$ cup light cream
2 teaspoons chopped parsley
    (for garnish)
croûtons (for garnish) –
    see box

Method
Trim and discard the roots and green tops from the leeks. Reserve 1 leek for garnish, split the remainder lengthwise, wash well and slice the white parts.

Melt the butter in a large saucepan, add the leeks and potatoes with the seasoning and cook over low heat, stirring, until they are almost soft. Cover with foil and the lid and cook 10 minutes or until very soft. Pour in the milk and water and stir until the mixture comes to a boil. Half cover with the lid and simmer 15 minutes. Work the soup through a sieve or food mill or purée in a blender.

Cut the reserved leek into fine slices, put it in cold water, bring to a boil and boil 2 minutes. Drain and pat dry with paper towels.

Reheat the soup; mix the egg yolks and cream in a bowl and stir in a little of the remaining soup and stir over low heat until the soup thickens slightly.

Watchpoint: do not let the soup boil or it will curdle.

Garnish the soup with a little sliced leek and chopped parsley. Serve the croûtons separately.

Pumpkin Soup

$1\frac{1}{2}$–2 lb pumpkin, peeled
3 medium potatoes, peeled
3 tomatoes, halved and seeded
5 cups cold water
salt and pepper
$1\frac{1}{2}$ tablespoons rice
little milk (optional)
1 tablespoon butter
$\frac{1}{4}$ cup heavy cream

Pumpkin is a member of the squash family, and it ripens later than the soft-skinned types of summer squash. If pumpkin is not available, the same soup can be made with fresh or frozen yellow squash. Serves 6–8.

Method
Cut the pumpkin into chunks, discarding seeds and fibers. In a kettle combine pumpkin, potatoes and tomatoes with the cold water and season. Cover, bring to a boil and simmer gently for 25–30 minutes or until the vegetables are tender.

Boil the rice in salted water for 12 minutes or until tender. Drain, rinse with hot water to separate the grains and reserve.

Work the soup through a sieve, or purée in a blender, and return it to the pan. Adjust the seasoning and add a little milk if the soup is too thick. Reheat it and add the rice, butter and cream. Stir well and serve.

Okra Pilaf

1 cup thinly sliced okra
4 slices of bacon
1 onion, chopped
$\frac{1}{2}$ green pepper, finely chopped
2 tomatoes, peeled, seeded
    and chopped, or 1 can ($8\frac{1}{4}$ oz)
    tomatoes
salt and pepper
1 cup rice

Method
Dice the bacon and fry it in a skillet until crisp. Take out with a slotted spoon and reserve. Fry the onion and pepper in the fat from the bacon until soft; add tomatoes and okra and cook, stirring occasionally, until soft and the liquid has evaporated. Season well with salt and pepper.

Meanwhile, boil the rice in plenty of salted water for 12 minutes, or until just tender; drain thoroughly. Combine the rice with the okra mixture, cover and cook in the top of a double boiler, or in a heatproof bowl over a pan of hot water, for 15 minutes or until the rice is thoroughly flavored with the tomato. Stir in the bacon just before serving.

Baked Summer Squash

1½ lb summer squash (any variety), sliced
1 medium onion, sliced
2 tablespoons oil
½ lb tomatoes, peeled and sliced
1 clove of garlic, crushed (optional)
1 teaspoon crushed dill seed
1 tablespoon chopped parsley
1 teaspoon sugar
salt and pepper
½ cup chicken stock

Method
In a skillet sauté onion in oil until soft. Arrange the squash in layers with tomatoes and cooked onion in a buttered baking dish, sprinkling each layer with garlic, herbs, sugar, and salt and pepper to taste. Pour on the stock and bake in a moderate oven (350°F) for 30 minutes or until the squash are tender.

Baked Winter Squash

2 medium butternut or acorn squash
¼ cup butter
¼ cup brown sugar
½ teaspoon ground cinnamon
½ teaspoon ground cloves
½ teaspoon ground allspice
½ teaspoon ground nutmeg

Method
Halve the squash and scoop out the seeds. Cut a slice from the base of each half so they sit firmly in place in a baking dish. In the center of each half put 1 tablespoon each of butter and sugar. Mix the spices together and add a pinch to the center of each half.

Bake in a moderate oven (350°F), basting often with the remaining butter, melted, and sugar for 40 minutes or until the squash are soft and brown.

The word **squash** is believed to have come from the Natick and Narraganset Indian *askúta-squash* meaning 'green thing eaten green'. Long before the first white men came to America, the Indians were growing a wide variety of this gourd plant. The two main types of squash — summer and winter — come in many different colors and shapes — and sizes range from quite small to mammoth specimens of enormous weight.

Poor Man's Caviar

1 large eggplant
¼ cup chopped parsley
1 clove of garlic, crushed
2 tablespoons vinegar
1 tablespoon lemon juice
1 tablespoon chopped mint
¼ teaspoon cinnamon
salt and pepper

Poor man's caviar is a Turkish dish, so called because it resembles the shiny gray color of caviar. Serve it as a dip or an appetizer with chunks of Syrian bread, or toasted white bread.

Method
Wipe eggplant and bake it whole in a moderate oven (350°F) for 1 hour or until soft. Let cool a little, halve it, remove the skin and finely chop the pulp. Beat in the remaining ingredients with salt and pepper to taste, pile it in a bowl and chill at least 2 hours before serving.

Stuffed Peppers

4 medium red or green peppers, cored and seeded
2 cups chicken stock, or tomato juice

Method
Set peppers in a deep baking dish and fill with one of the stuffings given below. Pour over stock or tomato juice, cover and bake in a moderate oven (350°F) for 45–60 minutes or until tender.

Mushroom and Rice Stuffing

2 onions, sliced
2 tablespoons butter
1 cup (¼ lb) chopped mushrooms
2 cups cooked rice
2 tablespoons chopped parsley
1 teaspoon oregano
salt and pepper

Method
In a skillet sauté the onions in the butter until soft. Add the remaining ingredients with salt and pepper to taste.

Corn Stuffing

2 cups cooked corn kernels
½ cup fresh white breadcrumbs
salt and pepper

Method
Combine corn with breadcrumbs and add salt and pepper to taste.

e scallop, two crookneck with zucchini on top, a butternut and acorn squash

Beef Stuffing

$\frac{3}{4}$ lb ground beef
2 tablespoons oil
1 onion, chopped
1 teaspoon thyme
$\frac{1}{2}$ teaspoon paprika
$\frac{1}{2}$ teaspoon chili pepper (or to taste)
1 cup stock
salt and pepper
1 cup cooked rice

Method
In a skillet heat oil and fry onion until soft. Add beef and cook, stirring, until brown. Add the thyme, spices, stock and salt and pepper to taste. Simmer 20 minutes or until all the stock is absorbed. Stir in the rice.

Creamed Corn

6 ears of fresh corn
6 tablespoons butter
$\frac{1}{4}$ cup heavy cream
salt and pepper

Method
Cut the kernels from the cob with a sharp knife or a corn scraper. Combine them in a pan with the butter, cream and seasoning. Cover and simmer 5–8 minutes or until the corn is tender, stirring occasionally.

Serve fresh corn on the cob with butter melting on top

Corn Mold

creamed corn, made with
  4 ears of corn, 3 tablespoons
  butter and 2 tablespoons
  heavy cream (see method,
  page 113)
2 tablespoons flour
1 cup milk
1 egg
2 egg yolks, beaten to mix
salt and pepper

Ring mold (1 quart capacity)

Method
Butter the ring mold.

In a saucepan melt 1 table-spoon butter, add the creamed corn and cook, stirring, until any liquid has evaporated.

In another pan melt the remaining butter, stir in the flour and, when foaming, pour in the milk. Bring the sauce to a boil, stirring constantly, season and simmer 2 minutes. Take from the heat and stir in the corn. Add the eggs and egg yolks, and season the mixture well. Pour into the prepared mold, cover with foil and set in a water bath. Bake in a moderate oven (350°F) for 25–30 minutes or until the mold is firm.

Take the mold from the water, let cool 2–3 minutes and turn out onto a platter.

Boiled Corn

Speed is essential when dealing with fresh corn. It should be eaten as soon as possible after picking, since the sugar content turns to starch within 24 hours. When young and tender it needs only 3–4 minutes cooking in boiling water. Add salt halfway through cooking to avoid toughening the corn. Drain it and serve at once with butter.

Succotash

2 cups fresh shelled baby lima
  beans
2 cups corn kernels
2 tablespoons butter
1 teaspoon sugar
$\frac{1}{4}$ cup water
salt and pepper
$\frac{1}{2}$ cup heavy cream

There are many short cuts to succotash, but none compares with that made with fresh corn and baby limas.

Method
Cook the beans in boiling salted water for 15–18 minutes or until tender. Drain, refresh under cold running water and combine in a saucepan with the corn, butter, sugar, water, and salt and pepper to taste.

Cook mixture over a low heat for 10–15 minutes and drain. Add the cream and heat thoroughly without boiling.

Corn Salad

2 cups cooked corn kernels
1 green pepper, cored, seeded
  and cut in thin strips
3 tomatoes, peeled and cut in
  wedges
$\frac{1}{2}$ cup vinaigrette dressing

Method
Blanch the pepper in boiling salted water for 1 minute. Drain and refresh under cold water. Mix with the corn and tomatoes and toss with the vinaigrette dressing.

If you like, reserve the tomatoes and spoon a little dressing over them separately, then arrange them around the edge of the salad bowl.

Corn Kernels
Fresh, frozen, or canned cooked corn kernels may be used in most recipes. Fresh kernels, which have the best flavor, are cut from the cob with a sharp knife and cooked until tender with a little milk and salt and pepper to taste. One ear of corn should yield about $\frac{1}{2}$ cup kernels. Frozen corn should be cooked according to package directions and drained; canned corn needs only to be drained.

Mushrooms Stuffed with Anchovy

5–6 (about 1 lb) medium
  mushrooms per person
6 fillets of anchovy, soaked
  in a little milk to remove
  excess salt
¼ cup butter
¼ cup fresh white breadcrumbs
clove of garlic, crushed
  (optional)
1 tablespoon chopped parsley
black pepper, freshly ground

Method

Drain the anchovy fillets and
chop them. Remove the stems
from the mushrooms and
chop finely.

Heat 2 tablespoons of the
butter and fry the chopped
mushroom stems until soft.
Take from the heat and stir
in the breadcrumbs, chopped
anchovies, garlic, if used,
parsley and black pepper.

Fill the mixture into the
mushroom caps and set in a
buttered baking dish. Dot the
mushrooms with the remaining butter, cover and bake in
a hot oven (400°F) for 12–15
minutes or until the mushrooms are tender.

Mushrooms and Onions à la Grecque

¾ lb mushrooms, quartered if
  large
16–18 small onions, peeled
1 cup white wine
1 cup stock
2 shallots, finely chopped
clove of garlic, crushed
2 teaspoons tomato paste
juice of 1 lemon
2 tablespoons olive oil
bouquet garni
salt and pepper

For garnish
1 tablespoon chopped parsley
1 lemon, thinly sliced

Method

In a shallow pan combine the
wine, stock, shallots, garlic,
tomato paste, lemon juice, oil,
bouquet garni and seasoning
and simmer 5 minutes.

Add the onions and simmer
15 minutes or until almost
tender. Add the mushrooms
and simmer 5 minutes longer.
Take out the vegetables and
put them in a glass bowl.

If necessary, boil the liquid
until it is reduced to 1 cup.
Let cool, then strain over the
vegetables.

Just before serving, sprinkle
the top with parsley and
arrange the lemon slices
around the edge of the dish.

Other Vegetables à la Grecque

Many other vegetables are
excellent cooked à la grecque;
use the same quantity of wine
mixture as for mushrooms and
onions à la grecque.

Artichokes: cut the stems
from 4 medium artichokes
and trim the leaves. Cook in
boiling salted water for
15–30 minutes, depending
on size, or until almost tender.
Pull the leaves from the artichoke bases and scoop out
the hairy chokes with a teaspoon, leaving the bottoms.
Cut the bottoms in quarters.
Simmer the bottoms in the
wine mixture for 8–10
minutes or until very tender.
Continue as for mushrooms
and onions à la grecque.

Frozen artichoke bottoms
or hearts can be cooked
directly in the wine mixture.

Carrots: trim and scrub 1
bunch of baby carrots or peel
and quarter 1 lb medium
carrots and cut in 3 inch
lengths. Simmer in the wine
mixture for 15–20 minutes or
until the carrots are tender.
Continue as for mushrooms
and onions à la grecque.

Cauliflower: divide 1 medium
cauliflower into sprigs and
simmer in the wine mixture
for 8–10 minutes or until
tender but still firm. Continue
as for mushrooms and onions
à la grecque.

Zucchini or yellow squash:
cut 1½ lb in ½ inch slices and
simmer in the wine mixture for
6–8 minutes or until just
tender. Continue as for mushrooms and onions à la grecque.

Cauliflower with Potato au Gratin

1 cauliflower, divided into
  sprigs
1 lb medium potatoes, thinly
  sliced
mornay sauce, made with
  1½ tablespoons butter,
  1½ tablespoons flour, 1 cup
  milk, ¼ cup grated Gruyère
  or dry Cheddar cheese,
  ½ teaspoon prepared
  mustard, salt and pepper
2 tablespoons butter
½ cup grated Gruyère or
  Parmesan cheese
  (for sprinkling)

Method

Parboil the potato slices in
boiling salted water for 8–10
minutes or until almost
tender; drain them. Cook the
cauliflower in boiling salted
water for 8–10 minutes or
until just tender, and drain.
Watchpoint: a bay leaf added
to the water will remove any
odor of cauliflower.

Arrange the potatoes overlapping in a shallow buttered
baking dish, and put the
cauliflower sprigs around the
edge.

Spoon the mornay sauce
into the center to coat the
potatoes. Dot the cauliflower
with butter, sprinkle the whole
dish with grated cheese and
bake in a moderately hot oven
(375°F) for 10–15 minutes or
until browned.

Cauliflower with potato au gratin is sprinkled with grated cheese and browned before serving (recipe is on page 115)

Provençal salad is a good accompaniment served cold with broiled steak or cold roast beef

Peperonata

6 red bell peppers, cored,
   seeded and cut in strips
2 medium onions, sliced
2 tablespoons oil
2 tablespoons butter
clove of garlic, crushed
salt and pepper
4 tomatoes, peeled, seeded
   and cut in wedges

Method
In a skillet fry the onions in
the oil and butter until lightly
browned. Add the bell peppers, garlic and seasoning,
stir, cover and cook gently for
10 minutes or until the peppers are almost tender.

Add the tomatoes and con-
tinue cooking for 25—30
minutes or until the tomatoes
are very soft. Taste for seasoning and serve hot or cold.

Provençal Salad

1 lb zucchini, trimmed and
   sliced
3 ripe tomatoes, quartered
2 red peppers, cored, seeded
   and sliced
2 green peppers, cored, seeded
   and sliced
6 tablespoons olive oil
2 shallots, or scallions,
   finely chopped
2 cloves of garlic, crushed
bouquet garni
black pepper, freshly ground

Serve cold with broiled steak
or cold roast beef.

Method
Set oven at moderate (350°F).

In a flameproof casserole
heat the oil, add the shallots
or scallions and cook slowly
until soft but not browned.
Add remaining ingredients,
season with pepper and cover
the pan. Bake in heated oven
for 30—40 minutes or until
the zucchini and peppers are
tender. Remove the bouquet
garni and cool.

117

Left, front: large brown soda bread, flat drop scones and buttered soda biscuits; behind: large white soda bread, soda biscuits, griddle scones, molasses biscuits and fly bread

How to make Quick Breads, Muffins, Biscuits and Scones

As the name suggests, quick breads are quick to make and offer a big return for very little effort. There is no waiting around, as with yeast breads; on the contrary, the quicker they are mixed, baked and eaten, the better they taste – this is particularly true of muffins and biscuits.

The leavening agents for quick breads, muffins and biscuits are basically the same, but the mixtures are all handled differently: biscuit dough is kneaded until it just holds together, muffin mixture should be stirred until thoroughly moistened but slightly lumpy, and the batter for quick breads is folded lightly but thoroughly until smooth after the flour is added.

119

Points to remember

The leavening agent for these mixtures is baking powder or a combination of baking soda with an acid ingredient like buttermilk, sour milk or sour cream. Soda and acid together release the carbon dioxide necessary to lighten the bread. In some recipes fresh milk is called for and twice the amount of cream of tartar to baking soda is added to release carbon dioxide. In this case 1 tablespoon of molasses, which is also an acid, helps rising.

All-purpose flour is generally used because the proportion of leavening agent needed is greater than the amount present in self-rising flour, which should not be used unless called for in the recipe.

Mixing. It's important to add the right amount of liquid; this may need to be adjusted depending on the flour. Biscuit dough should be soft and almost, but not quite, sticky; if too little liquid is added, finished biscuits will be hard and if too much liquid is added, dough will be difficult to handle. Muffin and quick bread mixtures should be just soft enough to fall from the spoon.

Handling. Biscuits and muffins must never be overworked. Knead biscuit dough only until it holds together, quickly roll or pat out with the knuckles and cut into wedges, circles or triangles. Stir muffins lightly until dough is just moistened.

In most quick breads, the liquid ingredients are added to the flour and the mixture is folded as lightly and quickly as possible until smooth.

Speed is essential in handling all quick breads, muffins and biscuits. Once the ingredients are combined, the chemical reaction starts releasing carbon dioxide. With 'double-acting' types of baking powder, the reaction is delayed but even so the mixture should be baked quickly for the leavening agent to have maximum effect.

Baking. Bake biscuits on floured but ungreased baking sheets. Biscuits and muffins are baked in a high oven (400°F–425°F) and quick breads are usually baked in a more moderate oven (around 350°F). In Britain a type of biscuit called a scone and some breads are cooked on top of the stove on a heavy metal griddle or in a skillet.

Storing. Biscuits and muffins are best eaten hot from the oven. Quick breads can be kept longer, particularly if they contain fat or fruit, but they are usually best eaten within 2–3 days.

Quick Breads

Soda Bread

4¾ cups flour
1½ teaspoons salt
1½ teaspoons baking soda
scant 3 tablespoons butter
about 2 cups buttermilk or
    2 cups fresh milk and
    2 teaspoons cream of tartar

This Irish bread can also be cooked on a griddle; for instructions, see page 127.

Method

Set oven at hot (400°F).

Sift flour with salt, baking soda and cream of tartar (if using fresh milk) into a bowl. Rub in butter with fingertips and mix in the buttermilk or fresh milk to make a soft dough. Turn dough onto a floured board and shape into a large round, about 2 inches thick.

Score deeply (about ¾ inch deep) into quarters, place on a floured baking sheet and bake in heated oven for 25–30 minutes or until the bread sounds hollow when tapped with your knuckles.

Fly Bread

Make as for soda bread, adding ½ cup currants to the sifted flour.

Brown Soda Bread

Make as for soda bread, but substitute 3 cups wholewheat flour for 3 cups of the all-purpose flour.

Deeply score soda bread into quarters with a knife

To test the soda bread, tap it sharply; when cooked it will sound hollow

Spoon Bread

1 cup white cornmeal,
    preferably water ground
2 teaspoons salt
2 cups boiling water
1 cup milk
4 eggs
5 tablespoons butter, melted

*Shallow baking dish (2 quart
    capacity)*

Spoon bread is a traditional accompaniment to baked ham and fried chicken.

Method

Thickly butter the dish and heat it in a hot oven (425°F).

Mix the cornmeal and salt in a bowl and stir in the boiling water until smooth. Let stand 5 minutes, then stir in the milk. Add the eggs, one by one, beating well after each addition.

Stir in the melted butter and pour the batter into the heated dish. Bake in heated oven for 25–30 minutes or until a skewer inserted in the center comes out clean. Serve at once, in the baking dish, with plenty of melted butter.

Pineapple Nut Bread

1 can (14 oz) crushed
    pineapple
1 cup chopped walnuts, or
    pecans
$2\frac{1}{4}$ cups flour
$\frac{1}{2}$ teaspoon salt
3 teaspoons baking powder
$\frac{1}{2}$ teaspoon baking soda
$\frac{3}{4}$ cup brown sugar
1 cup bran
1 egg
$\frac{1}{4}$ cup butter, melted

Large loaf pan (9 X 5 X 3 inches)

Method

Set oven at moderately hot (375°F). Grease the loaf pan.

Sift flour, salt, baking powder and baking soda together and mix with the sugar in a bowl. Add nuts and bran to these dry ingredients and make a well in the center. Beat the egg thoroughly and add to the flour mixture; add pineapple (with syrup from the can) and melted butter and stir until mixture is smooth.

Spoon the mixture into the prepared pan and bake in heated oven for 1 hour or until a skewer inserted in the center of the loaf comes out clean and the bread shrinks slightly from the sides of the pan. Cool slightly, then turn out onto a wire rack and cool completely.

Orange Currant Bread

$\frac{2}{3}$ cup orange juice
3 tablespoons grated orange
    rind
$\frac{1}{2}$ cup currants
2 cups flour
1 cup sugar
1 teaspoon baking powder
$\frac{1}{2}$ teaspoon baking soda
$\frac{1}{2}$ teaspoon salt
$\frac{1}{2}$ cup chopped pecans
1 egg
3 tablespoons melted butter

Large loaf pan (9 X 5 X 3 inches)

Method

Grease loaf pan and set oven at moderate (350°F).

Sift flour with sugar, baking powder, baking soda and salt into a bowl. Add currants and pecans. Beat the egg and stir in the orange juice and rind and melted butter. Make a well in the center of the dry ingredients, add egg mixture and stir until well blended. Spoon into the loaf pan.

Bake in heated oven for 50–60 minutes or until a skewer inserted in the center of the loaf comes out clean. Cool 10 minutes, turn out on a wire rack and cool completely.

Cranberry Orange Bread

2 cups, or 1 can (16 oz), whole
    cranberry sauce
juice and grated rind of 1 large
    orange
3 tablespoons butter
1 cup sugar
1 egg
3 cups wholewheat flour
2 teaspoons baking powder
1 teaspoon baking soda
1 teaspoon salt
$\frac{1}{2}$ cup wheat germ

Large loaf pan (9 X 5 X 3 inches)

Method

Grease loaf pan and set oven at moderate (350°F).

Cream butter, beat in sugar and continue beating until light. Beat in the egg with the orange rind. Mix flour with baking powder, baking soda and salt. Drain cranberries, pressing lightly to remove juice, reserve them and add the juice to the orange juice. Stir the juices into the butter mixture in three portions alternately with the dry ingredients. Stir in the cranberries and wheat germ and spoon the whole mixture into the prepared pan.

Bake in heated oven for 50–60 minutes or until a skewer inserted in the center of the loaf comes out clean. Cool slightly and turn out onto a wire rack to cool completely.

Walnut wholewheat bread is delicious cut in slices and spread with butter

Walnut Wholewheat Bread

1 cup walnut pieces
1 cup flour
2 teaspoons baking powder
1 teaspoon salt
$\frac{1}{2}$ teaspoon ground cinnamon
$\frac{1}{4}$ teaspoon ground nutmeg
$\frac{1}{2}$ teaspoon ground allspice
1 cup stone ground wholewheat flour
2 tablespoons shortening
$\frac{3}{4}$ cup sugar
1 egg, beaten to mix
1 cup milk

Large loaf pan (9 X 5 X 3 inches)

Method
Set oven at moderate (350°F) and grease the loaf pan.

Sift the regular flour with the baking powder, salt and spices. Stir in the wholewheat flour. Work the walnuts through the fine blade of a grinder or grind them with a rotary cheese grater.

Beat the shortening with the sugar until crumbly and stir in the egg. Stir the flour mixture into the egg mixture in three batches, alternately with the milk. Stir in the ground walnuts.

Pour the mixture into the prepared pan and bake the bread in the heated oven for 50–60 minutes or until a skewer inserted in the center comes out clean. Cool slightly and turn out onto a wire rack to cool completely.

Rock Cakes

2 cups self-rising flour
pinch of salt
$\frac{1}{2}$ cup butter
6 tablespoons sugar
$\frac{2}{3}$ cup golden raisins
3 tablespoons mixed chopped candied peel
2 eggs
1–2 tablespoons milk

The name of these small cakes refers not to their texture (they should be firm but crumbly), but to their jagged, uneven shape. Makes 24 cakes.

Method
Grease a baking sheet and set oven at hot (425°F).

Sift flour with salt into a bowl and rub in the butter with the fingertips until the mixture resembles fine crumbs. Stir in the sugar, raisins and peel. Whisk the eggs until frothy and stir into the dry ingredients with a fork, adding just enough milk to bind the ingredients together. Using a tablespoon, make mounds of the mixture on prepared baking sheet and bake at once in heated oven for 12–15 minutes or until brown and firm. Cool on a wire rack.

Watchpoint: the mixture should hold its shape — if too much milk is added, the cakes lose their rocky appearance.

Corn Sticks

1$\frac{1}{2}$ cups yellow or white cornmeal
$\frac{1}{2}$ cup flour
2$\frac{1}{2}$ teaspoons baking powder
1–2 tablespoons sugar
$\frac{3}{4}$ teaspoon salt
1 egg
2–3 tablespoons melted butter
$\frac{3}{4}$ cup milk

24 corn stick pans

Method
Thoroughly grease corn stick pans and set oven at hot (425°F).

Sift together flour, baking powder, sugar and salt into a bowl and stir in the cornmeal. Make a well in the center, beat the egg with the butter and milk and pour into the dry ingredients. Stir together as quickly as possible.

Heat the pans until very hot, spoon in the corn mixture and bake in heated oven for 15 minutes or until brown. Turn out onto a wire rack to cool.

Skillet Corn Bread

Make the batter as for corn sticks. Heat a heavy 10 inch skillet and bake the bread in a hot oven (400°F) for 30 minutes or until brown.

Muffins

Muffins should have unevenly rounded tops with a light crumbly consistency. If a muffin hardly rises and has a flat top with a peak in the center the oven temperature was too low; if the top is cracked and unsymmetrical the oven temperature was too high.

If the muffin is coarse-textured and full of tunnels the batter was over-mixed and the gluten in the flour developed to make the batter tough.

Plain Muffins

2 cups flour
3 tablespoons sugar
1 tablespoon baking powder
$\frac{1}{2}$ teaspoon salt
1 egg
$\frac{1}{4}$ cup melted butter
1 cup milk

10 muffin tins

Method
Grease tins and set oven at hot (425°F).

Sift flour with sugar, baking powder and salt into a bowl and make a well in the center. Beat egg with butter and stir into the milk. Pour into the flour mixture and stir together quickly until dry ingredients are moist but mixture is still rough. Spoon into the tins and bake in heated oven for 15–20 minutes or until well browned. Turn out on a rack to cool.

Date and Orange Muffins

To the plain muffin mixture, add $\frac{1}{2}$ cup chopped dates with the grated rind of 1 orange. Serve with orange marmalade.

Walnut and Honey Muffins

In the plain muffin recipe, eliminate the sugar and instead add $\frac{1}{4}$ cup honey to the egg mixture. Also use 2 tablespoons less milk. Add $\frac{1}{2}$ cup chopped walnuts, $\frac{1}{2}$ teaspoon ground cinnamon, $\frac{1}{4}$ teaspoon ground allspice and $\frac{1}{4}$ teaspoon ground nutmeg to the dry ingredients.

Fruit Muffins

In the recipe for plain muffins, substitute brown sugar for the granulated sugar and sour cream for the milk. Add 1 cup coarsely chopped fruit or if using fresh berries such as strawberries, halve them, if very large, and add to the batter.

A recipe for blueberry muffins was given in Volume 3.

Spiced Nut Muffins

$1\frac{1}{2}$ cups flour
$\frac{1}{2}$ cup sugar
2 teaspoons baking powder
$\frac{1}{2}$ teaspoon salt
$\frac{1}{4}$ cup shortening
$\frac{1}{2}$ cup milk
1 egg, beaten to mix

For nut filling
$\frac{1}{2}$ cup chopped walnuts, or pecans
2 teaspoons cinnamon
$\frac{1}{2}$ cup brown sugar
2 tablespoons flour
2 tablespoons melted butter

12 muffin tins

Method

Grease tins and set oven at moderately hot (375°F).

Sift flour, sugar, baking powder and salt together. Add shortening and cut in with a knife; rub with fingertips until mixture resembles fine crumbs. Stir milk into beaten egg, add to flour mixture and stir as lightly as possible until just mixed.

To make the nut filling: in a bowl combine the brown sugar, nuts, 2 tablespoons flour, cinnamon and melted butter. Spoon alternate layers of batter and nut mixture into the muffin tins, filling them two-thirds full, and bake in heated oven for 25 minutes or until muffins are brown. Serve hot with butter.

Bran Muffins

1 cup bran flakes
2 tablespoons shortening
3 tablespoons sugar
1 egg
$\frac{3}{4}$ cup milk
1 cup flour
2 teaspoons baking powder
$\frac{1}{2}$ teaspoon salt

12 muffin tins

Method

Grease tins and set the oven at hot (400°F).

Cream shortening, beat in sugar and continue beating until as light as possible. Beat in the egg. Stir in the milk, then bran flakes. Sift remaining ingredients together and stir into the bran mixture as lightly as possible until mixture is moist but still rough. Spoon into prepared tins and bake in heated oven for 20–25 minutes or until brown. Turn out on a rack to cool.

Quick Breads, Muffins, Biscuits and Scones

A delicious selection of breads, cakes and muffins that are easy to make (from left front, clockwise): rock cakes, orange currant bread, muffins, cranberry orange bread, corn sticks and rock cakes

Biscuits

Wholewheat Biscuits

2 cups wholewheat flour
2 cups all-purpose flour
½ teaspoon salt
2 teaspoons baking soda
2 teaspoons cream of tartar
4 teaspoons sugar
½ cup butter
1½ cups buttermilk, or 1½ cups fresh milk and 3 teaspoons baking powder

Makes 8 biscuits.

Method
Set oven at hot (425°F).

Sift the all-purpose flour with the salt, baking soda and cream of tartar into a bowl (with baking powder if using fresh milk). Add wholewheat flour and sugar and mix well. Rub in the butter with the fingertips until evenly distributed. Stir in the buttermilk or fresh milk and mix quickly to a soft dough.

Turn the dough onto a floured board, divide it in two, knead lightly and pat or roll it into 2 rounds, each about ¾ inch thick. Cut each round into four and place the pieces on a baking sheet, fitting them together again to make 2 rounds. Sprinkle with flour and bake in heated oven for 15–18 minutes or until the biscuits are brown.

Molasses Biscuits

2 tablespoons molasses
3 cups flour
½ teaspoon salt
1 teaspoon baking soda
1 teaspoon cream of tartar
¼ cup butter
¾ cup fresh milk

If you like, the milk in this recipe may be soured by adding 1 teaspoon lemon juice. Makes about 8 biscuits.

Method
Set oven at hot (425°F).

Sift flour with salt, baking soda and cream of tartar. Rub in butter with the fingertips until the mixture resembles crumbs. Stir the milk into the molasses and stir into the flour to form a soft dough.

Knead the mixture lightly on a floured board, then roll or pat out to about ¾ inch thick and cut into triangles. Bake in heated oven for 10–15 minutes or until the biscuits are lightly browned.

Molasses, the thick brown syrup that is separated from raw sugar during refinement, was probably first eaten by the Chinese and the Indians. Columbus introduced it to the West Indies and it became a very important part of colonial trade. In fact, until after the Civil War, it was the prime sweetener in America, used in doughnuts, baked beans, puddings, corn breads, cookies, cakes, or just poured over pancakes, muffins and hot buttered breads.

Soda Biscuits

3½ cups flour
1 teaspoon salt
2 teaspoons baking soda
6 tablespoons butter
1½ cups buttermilk, or fresh milk with 2 teaspoons cream of tartar

2 inch plain cookie cutter (optional)

Makes 30–32 biscuits.

Method
Set oven at hot (425°F).

Sift flour with salt, baking soda and cream of tartar (if using fresh milk), into a bowl. Rub in the butter with the fingertips until the mixture resembles crumbs. Add the buttermilk or fresh milk and mix quickly to a soft dough. Turn onto a floured board, knead lightly, then roll or pat out to about ¾ inch thick. Cut into 2 inch circles with the cookie cutter or cut into triangles.

Bake on a lightly floured baking sheet in heated oven for 15 minutes or until the biscuits have risen and are lightly browned.

Above: cut soda biscuits with a plain cookie cutter; make the trimmings into triangles

Below: take soda biscuits from oven when they have risen and are golden brown

Scones

Scones are the British equivalent of the American biscuit. Most are made from firm dough, like biscuits, but the mixture for others is a batter that bakes into a thick pancake called a drop scone. Both types are often cooked on a griddle.

Dough for cooking on a griddle should be a little thinner than the dough that is baked in the oven, or the outside crust will be too brown before the middle is done.

A griddle must be heated to the right temperature. A frequent mistake is to have it too hot at first, resulting in a burnt outside crust.

A good test is to sprinkle the griddle with flour; when this turns light brown in 3 minutes, the griddle is at the right temperature. Alternatively, sprinkle a few drops of water onto the griddle; when it is at the right heat, they will dance around. If possible, turn the biscuits or bread only once during cooking, but if the griddle was too hot in the first place, you will have to watch them carefully and they may need turning more than once.

A **griddle** is a thick metal plate used on top of the stove for making scones. pancakes, etc. The traditional griddle is a thick round iron plate with a semicircular handle, but some modern stoves come with a griddle which fits over a burner. Otherwise, a heavy skillet may be used.

Griddle Scones

2 cups flour
$\frac{1}{4}$ teaspoon salt
1 teaspoon baking soda
2 teaspoons sugar
$\frac{1}{4}$ cup butter
1 tablespoon currants (optional)
$\frac{3}{4}$ cup buttermilk and
   1 teaspoon cream of tartar,
   or $\frac{3}{4}$ cup fresh milk and
   2 teaspoons cream of tartar

Griddle, or heavy skillet

Makes 8 scones.

Method
Heat the griddle or skillet as directed above. Sift the flour with salt, baking soda and sugar into a bowl and rub in the butter with fingertips until the mixture resembles crumbs. Dissolve the cream of tartar in buttermilk or fresh milk. Add currants, if using, with buttermilk or fresh milk to the flour mixture and mix quickly to a soft dough.

Turn the dough onto a floured board, divide in half and shape into 2 rounds, $\frac{1}{2}$ inch thick; cut each round into quarters. Sprinkle these with flour and cook on the hot griddle or in the skillet for about 5 minutes or until they have risen and are lightly browned. Turn and cook for about 5 minutes on the other side. Split, butter and serve the scones at once.

Turn quartered griddle scones so they brown on both sides

Drop Scones

$1\frac{1}{4}$ cups flour
$\frac{1}{4}$ teaspoon salt
2 teaspoons baking powder
1 tablespoon sugar (or to taste)
1 egg
2 tablespoons melted butter
$\frac{3}{4}$ cup milk

Griddle, or heavy skillet

Makes 25–30 scones.

Method
Heat the griddle or heavy skillet over moderate heat while mixing the batter. Sift the flour, salt, baking powder and sugar into a bowl, make a well in the center and add the egg and melted butter. Stir to draw in the flour and add the milk gradually to make a smooth batter. Beat 1 minute.

Lightly grease the griddle or skillet and pour 3 inch circles of batter from a pitcher or the tip of a large spoon. As soon as the scones are puffed and full of bubbles, turn them over with a metal spatula — the cooked side should be golden brown. Brown the other side. Keep for a few minutes in a clean warm dish towel or serve at once with butter and honey or jam.

Potato Scones

$1\frac{1}{2}$ lb floury, freshly boiled potatoes
1 teaspoon salt (or to taste)
$1\frac{1}{2}$ cups flour

Griddle, or heavy skillet

Like drop scones, these are thin and flexible but they are different in shape and texture. Potato scones are made in large rounds marked in four parts, called farls, and are good eaten cold or fried with bacon for breakfast. Makes 12 scones.

Method
Work the potatoes through a ricer, or sieve them onto a floured board. Add salt to taste and work in the flour gradually, kneading lightly and carefully.

Divide the mixture into thirds and roll out each piece as thinly as possible into rounds the size of a dinner plate. Cut each round into quarters and bake the scones on a moderately hot griddle or skillet for 7–10 minutes until browned on both sides. Turn once only.

Set a Perfect Table

Traditions in table settings undoubtedly developed as a lesson in logic — the silver to be used first was placed farthest from the plate and nearest to the hand that would be holding it.

Interestingly enough, many of these 'rules' still apply although their interpretation is more relaxed. The entrée knife is placed at the right with the sharp edge facing the plate. The forks are arranged on the left of the plate in the order of usage. For example, if salad is served as the appetizer, as it is in some parts of the country, the salad fork is placed outside the dinner fork. When salad is served with the meal, or after the main course, the salad fork is next to the plate, all in logical fashion. Fork prongs are placed face up; ends of handles of all silver should be lined up about 1–1½ inches from the edge of the table. The spoons go on the right, hollow side up, in line with the knife, with the spoon that is to be used first at the outside of the line.

When bread and butter plates are used, they are placed 1 inch above the forks with the butter knife usually resting on the plate in a line parallel to the forks. Alternatively, the butter knife can be placed on top of the plate at right angles to the forks. This second arrangement looks best when the dessert spoon and fork are placed above the dinner plate (the European service now used by many people over here), with fork prongs facing to the right and bowl of dessert spoon facing to the left. Placing the spoon to the right or the left of the plate depends on whether the dessert is to be eaten with a fork or spoon — more comforting logic. The fork is always closest to the plate.

The traditional American dessert setting has the spoon and fork placed parallel to the other silverware, working in, in order of courses.

The water glass or goblet is placed 1 inch above the tip of the knife and is never filled more than two-thirds full. When wine is served, the wine glass — or glasses — assumes the position of the water goblet, which is displaced to the right.

The dinner napkin can be folded into a square or rectangle but, again, neatness is imperative. All edges of the linen should meet; all corners should join. The napkin can be placed to the left of the forks and in line with the forks, in other words, $1-1\frac{1}{2}$ inches from the edge of the table. Open edges, not the fold, should face toward the plate so that a corner of the linen can be picked up easily and the napkin unfolded on the lap with a minimum of flourish. The napkin can also be placed in the center of the dinner plate with the fold of the linen facing towards the knives — this is customary when formal place mats are used.

These are the traditional rules and regulations; but today there is great freedom in table service.

Brilliant color and bold design augment the classic all-white linen. Now there are cloths, mats and table runners in all colors, designs and textures to please any mood. If the fabric you like can't be bought already made into cloths and napkins, make your own. Use any fabric that takes your fancy as long as it is kept immaculately washed and ironed. Arrange the table with

geometric precision, keeping all the lines at right angles whenever possible by exactly placing the tablecloth or table mats.

For 'something in the center of the table' the traditional flowers and candles are still fine, as long as the decoration is low enough for you to see over and is not overwhelming in size. The candles should either be above or below eye level. Change the centerpiece

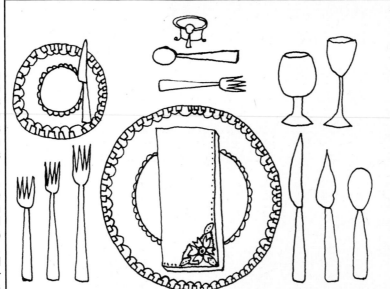

occasionally to vary the routine — use a handsome bowl of polished vegetables; a small potted plant or fern in a brass container; a crystal bowl filled with grapes of several varieties.

The table setting forecasts the food that is to be served, so review your dinner menu. An exciting variety of color and pattern in china and pottery can be interchanged during the same meal, one type for one course, another kind to use later on. Even silver can be changed about with the courses, the clean lines of contemporary design

with the main course, for example, and the lovely old silver you inherited for the dessert course. The few table traditions that we still observe remain a rule of the table simply because they make good sense in their own logical way.

Catering to the comfort of your guests is the only rule for buffet service. They should be able to walk around three sides of the table without crowding and they should

have a comfortable place to eat, either at a small table or from a tray.

Informal though it is, set the table, which should be as large as possible, carefully and creatively. Candle and flower decorations, if used, should be taller than usual, since they are viewed from above, but they must not overshadow the food.

The mood and drama of the table are up to you — use white damask or colored linens, or leave it bare, or use mats.

The menu must be simple but imaginative, requiring a

minimum of silver. All large casseroles, serving dishes, and platters should be arranged to balance each other on the table, with their serving spoons and forks placed nearby. Stack dinner plates near one of these serving dishes — whichever one you consider most important. Arrange the napkins in overlapping fashion near the plates; if you give frequent buffets, it is worth investing in large dinner napkins, because they are appreciated by guests.

The vertical-horizontal principle of regular table setting applies to buffet service, too. Forks should be lined up relatively close to the plates, about $1-1\frac{1}{2}$ inches from the edge of the table in neat rows, with the knives, if used. However, it is best to plan a menu where knives are not needed so one hand is left free to hold the plate. Silverware looks more attractive if it isn't made into a fancy arc or fan. Add a pepper grinder and salt cellar, or several of them, depending on the size of the party.

For salad, put a large bowl complete with serving utensils and salad plates at one side of the table so the guests can help themselves.

If the buffet table is a large one and there is plenty of room, line up glasses for ice water or wine. Otherwise, place them on a nearby serving table.

Nothing is less attractive than dirty dishes, so remove plates and platters as soon as they are empty and if possible, clear the table of all dishes and food before the dessert is served. Then arrange the dessert with the necessary plates and serving pieces on the clean table and let each guest help himself. Demitasses should be served by the hostess or an appointed guest.

KEEPING FOOD HOT

Luckily there are many simple and practical ways to keep food hot. The newest ranges have a cooking surface that completely covers the top and is thermatically controlled so that an inch one way or the other gives a scope in temperatures from the lowest simmer to intense heat.

Some foods wait more agreeably than others and there are dishes that even improve on standing and reheating.

Casseroles are an obvious example of this; almost all casserole dishes can be kept hot for $\frac{1}{2}$ hour or more; many will mellow in flavor if they are made 1–2 days in advance – particularly meat stews and ragoûts containing wine which should be reheated quickly on high heat for 10–15 minutes.

Vegetable soups and other good sturdy brews like bean soup all improve on standing. Baked beans and barley and most of the legumes are excellent after spending time in a warm oven, covered, of course.

Examples of the worst dishes to keep waiting are hot soufflés and baked Alaska. These dishes must be served at once. Steaks, chops and many broiled foods also taste better when served immediately. Dumplings, cheese dishes like Welsh rarebit, omelets, poached, fried and scrambled eggs cannot be kept hot and do not reheat satisfactorily. They all depend on a hot serving platter for the trip from kitchen to dining room if they are to be served piping hot. Deep or shallow fried foods in general lose much of their crispness while they wait. One solution, fairly effective but not perfect, is to drain the food well, arrange on a warm serving platter and keep it in a warm oven with the oven door open.

Several sauces such as Hollandaise and Béarnaise can be ruined by waiting. An effective way to keep them warm (and warm is the proper temperature, not hot), is to stand the saucepan in a bath of warm – not hot – water on the back of the stove.

Most au gratin dishes, which have been browned under the broiler, are not at their best after standing; however they can be prepared up to the point where the sauce is mixed in or spooned over, then reheated thoroughly, and broiled at the last minute to brown. And, of course, hamburgers, waffles and pancakes must be eaten almost from skillet and iron to be at their best.

The list of modern aids for keeping food hot grows longer by the year. Walk through any large housewares department and you will find trays and tables with heat-controlled tops as well as other things that have made life a lot simpler for the hostess. Among them are electric and non-electric casseroles of handsome design; plate-warming gadgets that keep a dozen plates at perfect temperature, looking somewhat like flannel accordions: thermatically controlled coffeemakers, bean pots, pot roasters, Dutch ovens, vegetable dishes, roll and French bread warmers. Even infants, from the moment they taste something other than milk, can have their food electrically heated in a three-sectional dish.

All these conveniences are nice to have but require lots of storage space in your kitchen and can be expensive. You can manage easily without them.

Plates heat beautifully in a warm oven. Bread and rolls can be wrapped in foil and heated in a warm oven. Use a double boiler or water bath for holding vegetables or creamy foods at the right temperature; just be sure to keep the water under the boiling point. If you stretch a piece of wax paper over the surface before the lid is set in place the creamy texture will hold. Keep in mind that most roasts of meat and poultry are easier to carve when they 'rest' at room temperature for 15–18 minutes. This gives a slight respite to the cook.

When food is served at the table or from a serving table, keep the dishes covered whenever possible. The covers hold in a surprising amount of heat. Serve hot biscuits bundled up in a napkin; to keep fresh asparagus as warm as possible, serve it on a linen napkin. And remember, the most elementary but prettiest of all ways to keep food hot is to place the warm platter over a candle warmer.

MEASURING & MEASUREMENTS

The recipe quantities in the Course are measured in standard level teaspoons, tablespoons and cups and their **equivalents are shown below.** Any liquid pints and quarts also refer to U.S. standard measures.

When measuring dry ingredients, fill the cup or spoon to overflowing without packing down and level the top with a knife. All the dry ingredients, including flour, should be measured before sifting, although sifting may be called for later in the instructions.

Butter and margarine usually come in measured sticks (1 stick equals $\frac{1}{2}$ cup) and other bulk fats can be measured by displacement. For $\frac{1}{3}$ cup fat, fill the measuring cup $\frac{2}{3}$ full of water. Add fat until the water reaches the 1 cup mark. Drain the cup of water and the fat remaining equals $\frac{1}{3}$ cup.

For liquids, fill the measure to the brim, or to the calibration line.

Often quantities of seasonings cannot be stated exactly, for ingredients vary in the amount they require. The instructions 'add to taste' are literal, for it is impossible to achieve just the right balance of flavors in many dishes without tasting them.

Liquid measure	Volume equivalent
3 teaspoons	1 tablespoon
2 tablespoons	1 fluid oz
4 tablespoons	$\frac{1}{4}$ cup
16 tablespoons	1 cup or 8 fluid oz
2 cups	1 pint
2 pints	1 quart
4 quarts	1 gallon

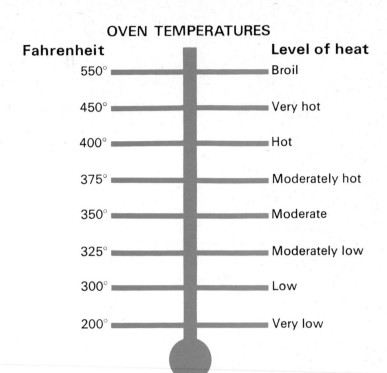

OVEN TEMPERATURES

Fahrenheit	Level of heat
550°	Broil
450°	Very hot
400°	Hot
375°	Moderately hot
350°	Moderate
325°	Moderately low
300°	Low
200°	Very low

OVEN TEMPERATURES AND SHELF POSITIONS

Throughout the Cooking Course, oven temperatures are stated in degrees Fahrenheit and in generally agreed levels of heat such as 'high' and 'moderate'. The equivalents are shown on the table above.

However, exact temperature varies in different parts of an oven and the thermostat reading refers to the heat in the middle. As the oven temperature at top and bottom can vary as much as 25°F from this setting, the positioning of shelves is very important. In general, heat rises, so the hottest part of the oven is at the top, but consult the manufacturer's handbook about your individual model.

Pans and dishes of food should be placed parallel with burners or elements to avoid scorched edges.

When baking cakes, there must be room for the heat to circulate in the oven around baking sheets and cake pans; otherwise the underside of the cakes will burn. If baking more than one cake in an oven that has back burners or elements, arrange the cakes side by side. If the oven has side burners, arrange cakes back and front.

Oven thermostats are often inaccurate and are unreliable at extremely high or low temperatures. If you do a great deal of baking or question the accuracy of your oven, use a separate oven thermometer as a check on the thermostat.

Cooking Curiosities

Pots and pans, spick and span. Gone are the days when kitchen drudges had to be employed to clean the enormous pans so beloved of chefs catering for large numbers in baronial halls or stately mansions.

The modern pot is light to handle, quick to cook with and easy to clean. It may be a bit of a chore to keep them sparkling but a well kept selection of crisply clean pots is still an indication of a craftswoman's respect for her basic tools. Looked at yours lately?

AN AMERICAN SCHOOL OF COOKERY FOR LADIES.

INDEX
(Volume 4)

G

E

JK

D

F

H

L

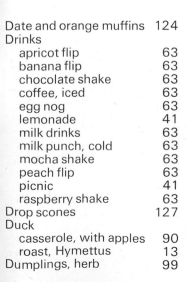

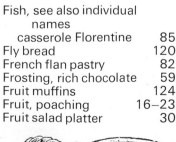

Acknowledgments

Photographs by Fred J. Maroon: pages 19, 34, 37, 41, 84, 112–113, 125. Other photographs by Michael Leale, John Cowderoy, Gina Harris, John Ledger and Roger Phillips. Photograph on page 117 by C. Délu/PAF.

NOTES

Notes